*Sports and
Physical
Education*

Sports and Physical Education

A Guide to the
Reference Resources

Compiled by
**Bonnie Gratch, Betty Chan,
and Judith Lingenfelter**

G P

Greenwood Press
Westport, Connecticut • London, England

Library of Congress Cataloging in Publication Data

Gratch, Bonnie.
  Sports and physical education.

  Includes indexes.
  1. Sports—Bibliography. 2. Physical education and
training—Bibliography. 3. Reference books—Sports—
Bibliography. 4. Reference books—Physical education and
training—Bibliography. I. Chan, Betty. II. Lingenfelter, Judith. III. Title.
Z7511.G7 1983 [GV704] 016.796 82-24159
ISBN 0-313-23433-7 (lib. bdg.)

Library of Congress Catalog Card Number: 82-24159
ISBN: 0-313-23433-7

First published in 1983

Greenwood Press
A division of Congressional Information Service, Inc.
88 Post Road West, Westport, Connecticut 06881

Printed in the United States of America

10 9 8 7 6 5 4 3 2 1

DEDICATION

Our work has been inspired by certain special individuals of the sports world. After having served as the host campus of the International Special Olympics of 1979, we were deeply moved by the commitment and achievement of these outstanding athletes. We are also pleased to note that finally, seventy years later, the International Olympic Committee has returned the two gold medals and restored the amateur status of one of the greatest all-around athletes in the world—the legendary Jim Thorpe. We dedicate this book to the memory of Jim Thorpe and to all those many Special Olympians throughout the world.

CONTENTS

ACKNOWLEDGMENTS

The authors wish to express their deep gratitude to several people. The staff at the Sport Information and Resource Centre of Ottawa, Ontario, deserve many thanks, particularly the director Gilles Chiasson and the information specialist Linda Wheeler, who patiently answered our several requests and made the collection available to us. Many colleagues at our own institution, the State University of New York, College at Brockport, deserve special thanks. Dr. Merrill Melnick of the Physical Education Department acted as our consultant, reviewed a part of this publication, and provided us encouragement. We owe a fond debt of gratitude to Peter P. Olevnik, Head of Reference, who supported our work with his unfailing understanding. We could never have undertaken this project without the able assistance of Robert Gilliam and Norma Lawrence of our interlibrary loan department, who never complained (well, *almost* never!) when we swamped them with our interlibrary loan requests. To Dr. George Cornell, our director, we extend our appreciation for his cooperation and support. We also wish to acknowledge the excellent work produced by our typist, Annabelle Day, and the editorial assistance of Paul Kobasa of Greenwood Press. Finally, whatever we have accomplished has been with the unconditional support of our respective families whose patience and understanding sustained us throughout this one and a half year process.

INTRODUCTION

PURPOSE

Reference sources for competitive sports have waxed and waned as certain sports have gained or lost popularity. Some have been fortunate enough to attract dedicated followers who have endeavored to meet the fans' insatiable demands for reference-type information on "their" sport (for example, *Baseball Register* or the *Encyclopedia of Football*). Other sports have not fared as well; they may receive only three pages of information buried within a general sports encyclopedia (for example, water polo). The literature on such allied fields as sports for the handicapped, sport psychology, and sports medicine, meanwhile, after years of benign neglect, is suddenly burgeoning forth with all manner of monographic and serial reference publications.

We three authors, academic reference librarians who serve a fairly large physical education clientele, asked each other if there was a way to organize the wealth of scattered information so that physical educators, sports practitioners, researchers, students, and librarians would actually know what is available. The result is this book. Like all tasks of this magnitude, what originally seemed manageable quickly became unwieldy. The scope has evolved through many discussions: we have tried to produce a broad-based guide to the reference resources in sports and physical education and certain allied fields, such as sports medicine, history of sports, women and sports, physical fitness, adapted physical education, sports for the handicapped, and the sociology, philosophy, and psychology of sport.

SCOPE

The scope of this guide includes English-language, United States, and Canadian monographic reference sources published since 1970, and ongoing North American, regularly published reference serial sources regardless of when they began publication. Reprints of pre-1970 reference sources that fall within the time scope have also been included. For some sports (for example, cricket, field hockey, and archery), English-language, non-North American publications are included because few or no United States or Canadian titles were identified. The reader will also notice that a few titles with pre-1970 publication dates are included. These have been included when more recent publications could not be identified for a particular sport.

The types of publications included are commercially published monographic and serial sources, ERIC documents, some United States and Canadian government publications, and some professional associations' reference publications. Admittedly, not all the professional association publications of a reference nature will be found here. We were more careful about locating such sources for certain sports for which fewer commercially published sources exist. Also, we have not tried to be comprehensive in including the membership directories of these professional associations.

Magazines and journals are not included unless their publishers produce annuals of a reference nature.

Reference serial sources are included only if we could verify that they had not ceased publication as of December 1981. In some cases, titles that we verified had ceased publication are included either because of the potential importance of the publication or because of the lack of other reference titles serving a similar function.

The identification of sports for inclusion is based primarily on those listed in the articles "Olympic Games" and "Winter Olympics" in Ralph Hickock's *New Encyclopedia of Sports* (New York: McGraw-Hill, 1977). Other major North American, competitive, spectator sports requiring physical ability have been added to the core list. Therefore, games like bridge or chess that require no physical ability are excluded, as are those in which participation, not competition, is the primary element. Children's games and sports are also excluded. Olympic equestrian sports and other competitive equestrian sports are included; all other sports employing animals are excluded. Also omitted are motor sports. Reference materials written for children, such as a sports dictionary, are not included.

Physical education and the allied fields of sports medicine, physical fitness, adapted physical education, sports for the handicapped, and the philosophy, psychology, and sociology of sport are within this guide's scope. Recreation and the subfield outdoor recreation are not included. Also omitted are reference works exclusively devoted to movement education, play, and leisure.

The authors have had to be selective for those sports within our scope. We have followed several guidelines.

For those sports that are performed both recreationally and competitively we have chosen reference works primarily on the basis of the competitive aspect of the sport. For example, if the main focus of a horse riding encyclopedia is its recreational aspects, it was not included in our section on "Equestrian Sports." If, however, a source detailing the recreational elements of the sport could be of potential use to individuals interested in the competitive aspects of the sport, we have included two or three titles to call attention to their existence. Examples of these would be directories of golf courses, tennis resorts, bicycle trails, and so forth.

For those sports where a large number of specific types of reference sources exist (for example, statistical sources for football or baseball), we have only included the more standard titles.

Within each sport or allied field category we have identified the following types of reference sources.

1. Bibliographical sources (that is, bibliographies, library catalogs, audio visual catalogs, and guides to the literature).

2. Biographical sources containing biographical information for twenty or more individuals. In some cases, however, sources containing less than twenty individuals are included if few or no titles published since 1970 could be located.

3. Catalogs of sports equipment.

4. Dictionaries (that is, glossaries and bilingual lexicons).

5. Encyclopedias (that is, multi-purpose sources that may include a variety of information, such as definitions of terms, biographical information, background articles, and statistics/records).

6. Directories and locational sources (that is, directories of organizations, manufacturers, suppliers, and guidebooks).

7. Statistical sources (that is, record books, listings of "champions," annuals, and registers of a primarily statistical nature).

8. Miscellaneous reference sources not falling into any of the other categories (that is, quotation books, sources for collectors of sports memorabilia, and so forth).

Rule books are also listed in a separate section, but because there are so many rule books for individual sports, we decided to include and annotate only those covering several sports, and to list the names and addresses of professional associations that publish rule books.

"Handbooks" and "guides" are generally not included because their focus is usually geared to technique and instruction. Some exceptions were made if these types of publications substantially included other information of a purely reference nature, or if for that sport, few other distinct reference sources were identified.

Reference sources oriented to a particular geographical subdivision, such as a state, province, or a region were excluded. Therefore, only those reference works covering the entire United States, Canada, or North America were considered for inclusion. Examples of those excluded would be a biographical dictionary of athletes in Ontario, or a directory of golf courses in the Southwest.

Similarly, we have omitted reference publications that focus on a particular team (for example, a biographical or statistical source for the New York Yankees) or conference (for example, a biographical or statistical source for the Big Ten Conference).

Obviously, certain sources are difficult to categorize. Although we have made these decisions to the best of our ability, the Subject Index provides additional access, since many other subject headings and publication format subheadings have been included there.

ARRANGEMENT

This work is organized into three parts. Part I, "Individual Sports," is an alphabetical arrangement of individual sports. In some cases sports are grouped, for example, boating sports, equestrian sports, tennis and racquetball, and so forth. If there are five or less reference sources for a particular sport, these are alphabetically listed by main entry and annotated. If six or more titles have been identified, they are subdivided by type of reference source, such as biographical sources or statistical sources, so long as there are at least two entries representative of a particular subdivision. If there are less than two entries for a particular category, they are grouped and located under the subdivision "Other."

Part II, "Sports and Physical Education: General and Topical," covers reference publications whose scope treats several sports, or those that deal with physical education in a general way. This part is arranged into general and topical sections. The general section subdivides by publication format (for example, bibliographical sources). Examples of sources within this section would be: encyclopedias of sports, directories of physical education programs, or biographical sources of athletes from many sports. Topical subdivisions have been created for those allied fields of physical education and sports for which we identified six or more entries. These topical subdivisions include: the history of sport; Olympic Games; physical education and sports for the handicapped; physical education and sports for other populations; medical, physiological, and physical fitness aspects of sports; psychology, sociology, and philosophy of sports; and the sports industry.

Part III, "Indexes, Data Bases, and Information Centers," includes descriptions of ongoing periodical indexing/abstracting services whose content scope include either an individual sport, or sports and physical education in general. Those services that provide computerized data bases are also described.

Chapter 33, "Information/Documentation Centers and Special Collections," identifies and describes North American information/documentation centers and substantially large special collections housed in university and public libraries.

Finally, the four indexes (Personal Author, Corporate Author, Title, and Subject) are keyed to the entry numbers in the *Guide*.

CONTENTS OF ENTRIES AND CITATION FORMAT

The entries are of two types: nonserial and serial. The citations for nonserial sources are composed of author(s)/editor(s), title, series note (if applicable), place of publication, publisher, date of publication, number of pages, and indication of the existence of illustrations, a bibliography, or an index, and the Library of Congress card number. A typical citation follows this format based on the 1977 *Modern Language Association Handbook*:

Winderbaum, Larry. *The Martial Arts Encyclopedia*. Washington, DC: Inscape Pub., 1977.   215p.   illus. bibl.   LC 76-43250.

Serial titles include the following bibliographic elements: title, author(s)/editor(s) (if editor does not vary from year to year), place of publication, publisher, frequency of publication, beginning date of publication (and ending date in some cases), an indication of the existence of illustrations, a bibliography, or an index, the ISSN number, and a note identifying the edition/year we examined. A typical citation follows this format:

Street & Smith's Official Yearbook: College Football. New York: Conde Nast. Annual.   1973- .   illus.   ISSN 0091-9977.

In some cases titles for serials have changed over the years. We decided to list the date the serial began publication, even if at that time it had a different title, so that the reader could better gauge the continuity of a particular source. The title changes are noted within the annotation.

Abbreviations used and descriptions of other types of numbers that might be listed in parentheses at the end of a citation are as follows:

SIRC # —This is the classification number assigned to a document housed in the Sports Information Resource Centre (SIRC) in Ottawa, Ontario. This number is included only if the document is an unpublished source, and therefore difficult to verify and obtain. SIRC makes its material available through interlibrary loan networks.

ERIC ED # —This is the accession number assigned by the Educational Resources Information Clearinghouse (ERIC). These materials are available for purchase or for loan via interlibrary loan networks.

SUDOC # —This abbreviation represents the Superintendent of Documents number, a classification system used by the U.S. Government for its publications. These materials may be available for purchase or for loan via interlibrary loan networks.

We attempted to examine all sources included so that we could verify bibliographic information and prepare the descriptive annotations. For the small number of sources we were unable to examine, we based our annotations on secondary sources such as reviews and annotated bibliographies. A statement identifying the date of the secondary source used follows these annotations. Only a handful are included without annotations.

RESOURCES USED TO IDENTIFY APPROPRIATE MATERIALS

The identification of appropriate materials for inclusion was accomplished by searching specialized bibliographies and such standard tools as:

American Reference Books Annual (ARBA). Littleton, CO: Libraries Unlimited, 1970-1982.

Cumulative Book Index. New York: Wilson, 1970-1981.

Dictionary Catalog of the Applied Life Sciences Library. University of Illinois at Urbana-Champaign. Boston, MA: G. K. Hall, 1977.

Directory of Directories. Detroit, MI: Gale, 1980.

Irregular Serials and Annuals: An International Directory. 6th and 7th ed. New York: Bowker, 1980, 1982.

Library of Congress Catalogs—Subject Catalogs. Washington, DC: Library of Congress, 1970-September, 1981.

Marshall, Joan K., comp. *Serials for Libraries*. Santa Barbara, CA: ABC-Clio, 1979.

Monthly Catalog of U.S. Government Publications. Washington, DC: U.S. Government Printing Office, 1970-1981.

Sheehy, Eugene P. *A Guide to Reference Books*. 9th ed. and *Supplement to 9th ed*. Chicago, IL: American Library Association, 1976, 1980.

Sport Bibliography. 8 vols. Ottawa, ONT: Sport Information Resource Centre, 1981.

Subject Guide to Books in Print 1981-82 and *Books in Print Supplement 1981-82*. New York: Bowker, 1981, 1982.

In addition, we also carried out computer searches of the ERIC data base, the *Monthly Catalog of U.S. Government Publications* data base, and the SIRC data base. The latter data base is a product of the Sport Information Resource Centre, Ottawa, Ontario, and reflects their outstanding collection of materials in all fields of physical education and sports. Some of our research and actual examination of materials was accomplished at this information center.

A greater representation of United States publications will be evident because Canadian national bibliographies and catalogs were not consulted. Such a lack is not a careless omission, but rather a deliberate decision to restrict the project to manageable limits. We are fully aware, however, of the richness of Canadian-published reference sources in these fields. We look forward to another publication that will more accurately reflect Canadian and other English-language reference sources.

PART I
INDIVIDUAL SPORTS

1.
ARCHERY

1. Bobbs, Howard, and Marcia M. Miller. <u>Bows and Arrows: An Archery
   Bibliography</u>. 1st ed. Sante Fe, NM: Sunstone Press, 1974. 22 p.
   LC 74-188830.

   A list of 211 unannotated titles arranged in alphabetical order by
   author. Most are in English, a few from the late 15th century. Also
   includes French, German and Danish publications.

2. Hougham, Paul C. <u>The Encyclopedia of Archery</u>. So. Brunswick, NJ:
   A.S. Barnes, 1958. 202 p. illus. index. LC 57-9910.

   The introductory chapter explains the nomenclature of the bow, bow-
   string and arrows. Main section includes records of tournaments,
   rules of safety, associations, and a list of shops and suppliers.

3. Lake, Fred, and Hal Wright. <u>A Bibliography of Archery</u>. Manchester,
   ENG: Simon Archery Foundation, 1974. 501 p. index. LC 74-183076.

   A list of 5000 articles, books, films, manuscripts, theses, etc. on
   hunting and recreational uses of the bow from earliest times to 1972.
   Arranged alphabetically by author, then chronologically by titles,
   it includes foreign language material. Locations given for U.K.,
   U.S. and Canadian libraries where publications available.

4. Rhode, Robert J., and Arlyne Ruhl. <u>Archery Champions</u>. 3rd ed. Min-
   neapolis, MN: Robert Rhode, 1968. 112 p. illus.

   An authoritative record of top scores in international, national target and national field tournaments. Also biographies of outstanding
   champions and their shooting techniques.

2.
BASEBALL

Since there are so many statistical sources of a reference nature for baseball, only the more standard, commercially published ones are listed as representative of this type. Even with the preceding limitation the reader might observe the seemingly apparent duplication. Although much of these data are duplicated in some of the sources, arrangement and access points are usually different from source to source. Notably lacking are the league and professional association statistical publications and registers. These can best be identified by inquiring with the specific association or league of interest. Registers and "encyclopedias" that are chiefly statistical in content are grouped under the heading "Statistical Sources" even though some of them also provide biographical information on career performance. Excluded are those annuals for which no information could be obtained regarding current publishing activity.

BIOGRAPHICAL SOURCES

5. Allen, Maury. Baseball's 100: A Personal Ranking of the Best Players in Baseball History. New York: A & W Visual Library, 1981. 316 p. illus. LC 80-70369.

   Brief biographical sketches with photos of the author's choice of best players selected from baseball history.

6. Appel, Martin and Burt Goldblatt. Baseball's Best: The Hall of Fame Gallery. Updated 1980 ed. New York: McGraw-Hill, 1980. 439 p. illus. LC 80-12628.

   One to two page anecdotal sketches of all the persons elected to the Baseball Hall of Fame up through the 1979 inductees. Photos accompany each article.

7. Broeg, Bob, ed. Super Stars of Baseball: Their Lives, Their Loves, Their Laughs, Their Laments. St. Louis, MO: Sporting News, 1971. 329 p. illus. LC 79-26472.

Life stories with playing records of 40 baseball greats from Honus
Wagner to Stan Musial.

8. Davis, Mac. Hall of Fame Baseball. Cleveland, OH: Collins World,
    1975. 146 p. illus. index. LC 72-9966.

    Biographical articles from 1 - 3 pages about 33 Hall of Fame immor-
    tals. Statistical records included.

9. Karst, Gene, and Martin J. Jones. Who's Who in Professional Base-
    ball. New Rochelle, NY: Arlington House, 1973. 919 p.
    LC 73-11870.

    Arranged alphabetically, this provides biographical sketches for
    some 1,500 players, managers, coaches and other officials.

10. Murray, Tom, ed. Sport Magazine's All-Time All Stars. New York:
    Atheneum, 1977. 454 p. LC 76-53400.

    Approximately 20 page-long biographies for 22 of the best players
    from the beginning days of baseball to the 1970's. Biographies
    written by writers for Sport Magazine. Players included are repre-
    sentative of all playing positions.

11. National Baseball Hall of Fame and Museum. Cooperstown, NY: The
    Museum, 1978. 70 p. illus. LC 76-377108.

    Brief biographical sketches of Hall of Fame members, a sketch of the
    history of the Cooperstown National Baseball Hall of Fame and Museum,
    and lifetime records of members comprise this paperback publication.
    Many photographs, especially of Museum exhibits.

12. Ritter, Lawrence, and Donald Honig. The 100 Greatest Baseball Play-
    ers of All Times. New York: Crown, 1981. 273 p. illus. index.
    LC 80-23046.

    One to two page sketches of 100 players who "played the bulk of their
    games after 1900" and maintained high levels of achievement through-
    out their career. Many photographs.

STATISTICAL SOURCES

13. Cohen, Richard M., and David S. Neft. The World Series: Complete
    Play-by-Play of Every Game, 1903-1978, Box Scores of Every Game,
    Records of Every Participant, All-Time Series Records and Leaders.
    New York: Dial Press, 1979. 416 p. illus. LC 79-4576.

    Paperback including for each World Series: a description of key
    events of the season, high points of the Series, box scores, and
    inning-by-inning detail for each batter. Final section has composite
    data listed in various categories -- slugging averages, team perfor-
    mance, etc.

14. The Complete Handbook of Baseball. Ed. by Zander Hollander. New
    York: New American Library. Annual. 1970-   . illus.

    Arranged by professional team, this is a guide to the profiles and
    statistics of "key" players in both leagues. Other sections list
    major league year-by-year leaders, world series summary, all time
    records, and schedules for the current season. Duplicates informa-
    tion in Sporting News' Guide and Register. (1980 ed. examined.)

15. Davenport, John W. Baseball Graphics. Madison, WI: First Impres-
    sions, 1979. 152 p.

    In over 200 graphs, from bar graphs, to bell curves, to shapes and
    forms and colors, this creative work provides major league pennant
    races, batting and pitching feats, team histories, and World Series
    heroics in graphic forms.

16. MacFarlane, Paul, ed. Daguerreotypes of Great Stars of Baseball.
    Rev. ed. St. Louis, MO: The Sporting News, 1981. 320 p. illus.
    index. LC 81-144698.

    A jam-packed source for the lifetime records of 432 baseball greats
    from the first year of official league play in 1876 to 1980. All
    Hall of Fame members are included, as well as those players with
    either a lifetime batting average of .300, 2,000 hits, 200 homers,
    175 pitching victories, or 2,000 strikeouts. Photographs of players
    accompany each entry, plus a 32 page section of photographs. Player
    index at end of volume.

17. Neft, David S., Richard M. Cohen, and Jordan A. Deutsch. The Com-
    plete All-Time Pro-Baseball Register. Rev. ed. New York: Gros-
    set and Dunlap, 1979. 352 p. LC 79-127172.

    Described as the portable, more economically priced "companion" to
    the Sports Encyclopedia: Baseball. Arranged in four chronological
    periods, it provides facts and records for batting and pitching from
    1901 through 1978.

18. Neft, David S., Richard M. Cohen, and Jordan A. Deutsch, eds. The
    Sports Encyclopedia: Baseball. 3rd ed. New York: Grosset and
    Dunlap, 1981. 526 p. LC 73-15137.

    With data complete through the 1980 season, this source arranges its
    records and statistics by time periods from 1901-1919 to 1973-1980.
    Each time period is preceded by a one page summary of major league
    action in that period and then briefer summaries of individual sea-
    sons follow with detailed team rosters and statistics. Final sec-
    tion lists data for many categories of single-season and lifetime
    leaders. No index to access data by player's name. Not as compre-
    hensive as the Baseball Encyclopedia (#26).

19. Official Baseball Dope Book. St. Louis, MO: Sporting News. An-
    nual. 1942-   . illus. ISSN 0162-5411.

A general compendium of data and rosters. Includes diagrams of ball parks and attendance figures for American and National League stadiums; All-Star Game records; averages, and box scores of Championship Series; listing of executives of baseball and the major league clubs; spring training rosters and the players' previous year's important statistics. (1980 ed. examined.)

20. Official Baseball Guide. St. Louis, MO: Sporting News. Annual.
     1942-   . index. illus. ISSN 0078-3838.

Comprehensive source of data and statistics for the previous year's season. Complete statistics for American and National Leagues including day-by-day scores, official averages and team photos. Nearly complete for the minor leagues, listing major batting, fielding, and pitching statistics. Review of previous season's All-Star Game, World Series, and Championship Series. Year-end leaders listed in categories. (1981 ed. examined.)

21. Official Baseball Record Book. St. Louis, MO: Sporting News. Annual. 1972-   . ISSN 0078-4605.

Continues One for the Book (1949-1971). For the categories batting, pitching, base stealing, and fielding, every major league record for individuals and teams is provided from 1901 through the latest season. (1981 ed. examined.)

22. Official Baseball Register. St. Louis, MO: Sporting News. Annual.
     1940-   . illus. ISSN 0067-4281.

This annual complements the other five Sporting News's baseball publications devoted to records and statistics, since it presents alphabetically by name statistical data for active players and major league managers and coaches, as well as resumes of the players' awards and brief biographical data. Batting, pitching and fielding statistics listed by year. (1981 ed. examined.)

23. Official National Collegiate Athletic Association Baseball Guide.
     Shawnee Mission, KS: National Collegiate Athletic Assn. Annual.
     1958-   . illus.

Statistics, previews and reviews of the collegiate baseball scene for each season. All-American teams listed for each division and rules and rule changes provided. Some photographs. (1980 ed. examined).

24. Official World Series Records: Complete Box Score of All Games,
     1903-1980. St. Louis, MO: Sporting News. Annual. 1953-   .
     index. ISSN 0078-3900.

In addition to the complete records, year by year, from 1903 up to the latest edition, this pocket-size manual includes shut-out games, home runs, attendance and financial figures, umpires, and a wide range of batting, fielding, pitching, and other records for individual players and clubs. (1981 ed. examined.)

25. Paretchan, Harold R. The World Series: The Statistical Record.
     Rev. ed. So. Brunswick, NJ: A.S. Barnes, 1974. 351 p.
     LC 72-5181.

In 88 separate tables, a comprehensive statistical history is presented for World Series records from 1903 through 1973. Part I's
tables present data for players driving in winning or decisive runs.
Individual offensive records make up the tables in Part II, and individual home run records are the subject of Part III tables.

26. Reichler, Joseph L., ed. The Baseball Encyclopedia: The Complete
    and Official Record of Major League Baseball. 5th ed. Rev. and
    expanded. New York: Macmillan, 1982. 2248 p. LC 82-167.

Considered the "bible" of baseball because it is the official au-
thority for statistical data for the National and American Leagues.
This revised ed. updates the material through the completion of the
1981 season. Introductory section on history of baseball is followed by sections listing: special achievement, records, and
awards; lifetime major league rosters; all-time leaders; teams and
their players; registers by national association, manager, player,
and pitcher; the World Series; all-star games. "Player Register"
is the longest of the sections and provides basic facts about each
player plus his year-by-year batting records.

27. Reichler, Joseph L. The Great All-Time Baseball Record Book. New
    York: Macmillan, 1981. 544 p. illus. index. LC 81-182.

Unusual and generally unrecorded statistics and facts from the beginning of major leagues through 1980. Sections for a variety of
individual batting, pitching, and fielding records; rookie records,
and team records for such things as brother batteries, most wins
and losses, best lefty-righty duos, etc. Player index at end lists
the notable facts under each person's name.

28. Siwoff, Seymour, ed. The Book of Baseball Records. Rev. ed. New
    York: Seymour Siwoff, 1981. 380 p. index. LC 72-622841.

This compilation of records updates the 1972 ed. which continued
The Little Red Book of Major-League Baseball (1926-71). Arranged
in 4 sections, Regular Season, World Series, Championship Series,
and All-Star Games, it provides records in batting, pitching and
fielding. Additional tables of baseball's most spectacular feats.

29. Street & Smith's Official Yearbook: Baseball. New York: Conde
    Nast Pub. Annual. 1941-   . illus. ISSN 0491-1520.

Provides records, brief biographical sketches, rankings, and schedules for professional baseball's prior year's season. (1980 ed.
examined.)

30. Thompson, Sherley. All-Time Rosters of Major League Baseball
    Clubs. Rev. ed. by Pete Palmer. So. Brunswick, NJ: A.S. Barnes,
    1973. 723 p. LC 73-156.

Revision of 1967 ed. Coverage includes club records and yearly rosters. Each player's entry contains nickname, weak and strong
points, and records. For statistics alone, Baseball Encyclopedia
(#26) or Official Baseball Register (#22) are preferable.

31. Turkin, Hy, and S. C. Thompson. The Official Encyclopedia of Base-
       ball. Revised by Pete Palmer. 10th rev. ed. So. Brunswick, NJ:
       A.S. Barnes, 1979. 668 p. illus. LC 78-68004.

     Although this work lacks the depth of The Baseball Encyclopedia
     (#26), it is a standard complement to it. Chapters on history,
     registers of all players' records since 1871, special records,
     honored players, administration, miscellany, and stadium diagrams.

OTHER

32. Grobani, Anton. Guide to Baseball Literature. Detroit, MI: Gale,
       1975. 363 p. index. LC 74-17223.

     A classed bibliography divided into 33 chapters on various aspects
     of baseball -- histories, instructional manuals, rule books, bio-
     graphies, etc. Includes citations to books, articles and pamphlets
     published in U.S. from early 19th century through 1972. Brief de-
     scriptions accompany citations. Title index only.

33. Grosse, Philip. Le Baseball: Anglais-Francais. Scottsdale, AZ:
       Philip Grosse, 1980. 23 p. (ERIC ED 200 045).

     One of three pamphlet, bilingual glossaries on this ERIC document.
     Alphabetical listing of about 300 words and phrases related to base-
     ball and the French equivalents.

34. Grosse, Philip. Baseball-Beisbol: Spanish-English. Scottsdale,
       AZ: Philip Grosse, 1980. 24 p. (ERIC ED 192 547).

     Alphabetical English-Spanish listing of more than 300 words, phrases,
     and sentences related to baseball as it is reported in Mexico City
     or in Spanish language newspapers in the U.S.

35. Merkel, Paul, comp. Bibliography of Baseball Films and Publica-
       tions. Hamilton Square, NJ: U.S. Baseball Federation, 1980.
       98 p.

     Arranged by topics, this bibliography lists films and books (some
     out of print) alphabetically by author/producer. The Coaching and
     Teaching Aids Committee of the American Assn. of Baseball Coaches
     calls this "the most complete bibliography on baseball books and
     films."

36. Scholl, Richard. Running Press Glossary of Baseball Language.
       Philadelphia, PA: Running Press, 1977. 94 p. illus. LC 77-410.

     Another in the Running Press series of glossaries, this paperback
     has more than 800 entries for baseball terminology and jargon of
     use to both novices and professionals.

37. Shannon, Bill, and George Kalinsky. The Ballparks. New York:
       Hawthorn Books, 1975. 276 p. illus. index. LC 75-5035.

Of borderline reference use, this unique source tells the detailed history of 26 stadiums. Arranged alphabetically by stadium. Many photographs interspersed with text. Appendices give ballpark diagrams and seating capacities; attendance records; first and last game scores and dates for all teams in all parks; franchise locations; and a list of minor league ballparks.

38. Society for American Baseball Research - Membership Directory.
     Cooperstown, NY: Society for American Baseball Research. Annual.
     19? -   .

Alphabetically arranged, name, address, phone, occupation, and baseball interests are listed for about 800 people. Available to members only. (Based on 1980 secondary source.)

3.
BASKETBALL

BIOGRAPHICAL SOURCES

39. Basketball Stars. New York: Pyramid Books. Annual. 19?- .
    illus. ISSN 0585-0258,

    Overall descriptions of the season. Pro team's section precedes the
    main part of the work, which are alphabetical-by-player articles de-
    scribing the performance of each player. (1979 ed. examined.)

40. Mendell, Ronald L. Who's Who in Basketball. New Rochelle, NY: Ar-
    lington House, 1973. 248 p. LC 73-11871.

    Over 900 brief biographical sketches of pro and college players,
    coaches and officials from 1891 to 1973. Alphabetically-by-name,
    but no cross references.

41. Padwe, Sandy. Basketball's Hall of Fame. Englewood Clifss, NJ:
    Prentice-Hall, 1970. 193 p. illus. LC 76-99451.

    Written with the cooperation of the Basketball Hall of Fame, this
    is the official account of the Hall of Fame. Fifteen chapters cover
    all-time great basketball innovators and personalities, with a fi-
    nal chapter covering biographical data and photographs of Hall of
    Fame members.

42. Prep All-American Basketball Yearbook. Montgomery, AL: Coach &
    Athlete. Annual. 196?- . illus. ISSN 0098-2490.

    This annual provides brief biographical data on the most outstanding
    high school basketball players each year. (1975 ed. examined.)

DICTIONARIES/ENCYCLOPEDIAS

43. Hollander, Zander, ed. The Modern Encyclopedia of Basketball. 2nd
    rev. ed. Garden City, NY: Dolphin Books, 1979. 624 p. illus.
    index. LC 78-22636.

Concentrating on the modern era (from mid-1930's), this source is considered a standard work on college and professional basketball. Chapters combine lengthy articles and statistics. Also included are chapters on the Olympics and high school champions. New to this edition are the chapters on collegiate women's basketball and one on junior college competition. Season and career records of every player in NBA and ABA history complete the work. Appendixes provide rules and list of basketball books in print.

44. Hollander, Zander, ed. The NBA's Official Encyclopedia of Pro Basketball. New York: New American Library, 1981. 532 p. illus. index. LC 81-82815.

The title is slightly misleading, since this is the updated and expanded version of Hollander's Pro Basketball Encyclopedia (1977) and also because articles and statistics for the ABA are also included. Lengthy articles document basketball from its advent. Biographical sketches of the "greatest" players and Hall of Fame inductees are provided along with year-by-year records for more than 1,800 players in the "All-Time Players" section.

45. Liss, Howard. Basketball Talk for Beginners. Illustrated by Frank Robbins. New York: J. Messner, 1970. 95 p. illus. LC 72-123163.

Sportswriter Howard Liss provides clear, simple explanations of both basketball slang and the rules of the game. More than 50 diagrams and drawings illustrate court action.

STATISTICAL SOURCES

46. Basketball Guide. Ed. by Jack Clary. Clearwater, FL: Snibbe Pub. Annual. 1971- . ISSN 0079-5518.

Formerly titled Pro Basketball Guide, this provides NBA and ABA rosters, records, schedules and statistics. (Based on 1980 secondary source.)

47. The Complete Handbook of Pro Basketball. Ed. by Zander Hollander. New York: New American Library. Annual. 1974- . illus.

Each year's edition provides extensive player histories and statistics and records for individual players arranged team by team. NBA all-time records and schedule also provided. (1980 ed. examined. Statistics only for the NBA were found in this ed.)

48. National Basketball Association Official Guide. St. Louis, MO: Sporting News. Annual. 1958- . illus. ISSN 0078-3862.

Complete picture of NBA statistics since the League's organization in 1946. Each year's edition presents records, statistics and career information for the prior season. Also includes rules, current team rosters, schedules, and information on the Hall of Fame. (1980-81 ed. examined.)

49. National Collegiate Athletic Association: Basketball. Shawnee
      Mission, KS: National Collegiate Athletic Association. Annual.
      19? -   . illus.

      This annual guide offers comprehensive treatment for the college
      basketball season. Two sections -- "Previews-Reviews" and "General
      Reviews" contain descriptions and data summarizing and predicting
      each NCAA team's performance. Player records provided for NCAA
      championship participants. Season's schedules complete the source.
      (1981 ed. examined.)

50. Neft, David S., R. T. Johnson, and R. M. Cohen. The Sports Encyclo-
      pedia: Pro Basketball. New York: Grosset & Dunlap, 1975. 368 p.
      LC 74-7552.

      Similar to the other two titles by Neft on baseball and pro foot-
      ball, this source presents a complete statistical history of pro-
      fessional basketball for the years 1891-1974. Comprehensive records
      for the teams and players are arranged into time periods which cor-
      respond to the formation and influence of professional basketball
      leagues and associations.

51. Official American Basketball Association Guide. St. Louis, MO:
      Sporting News. Annual. 1968-197?. illus. ISSN 0078-382X.

      Similar to its companion, National Basketball Association Official
      Guide, this annual guide provided current club schedules and ros-
      ters, yearly standings, statistics and playoff results, as well as
      complete coverage of ABA statistics since the league began in 1964.
      Ceased in mid 1970's. (1975-76 ed. examined.)

52. Official National Basketball Association Register. St. Louis, MO:
      Sporting News. Annual. 19? -   . illus. ISSN 0271-8170.

      Supplementary to the NBA Official Guide, this source is player-
      oriented. Alphabetical listing by player which provides career
      records for all players who were in at least one game in the season
      covered by each edition. Also has a year-by-year summary of the
      East-West All-Star Game since its 1951 inception. (Based on 1981
      secondary source.)

53. Street and Smith's Official College, Pro, and Preparatory Yearbook:
      Basketball. New York: Conde Nast. Annual. 1970-   . illus.
      ISSN 0092-511X.

      This title continues Street and Smith's College and Pro Official
      Yearbook: Basketball. Analyzes and evaluates basketball for col-
      lege, pro, and prep school fans, and provides complete coverage, in-
      cluding schedules, ratings, prediction, and photos. (1979 ed. exa-
      mined.)

OTHER

54. Davis, Gwendolyn C. <u>An Annotated Bibliography on the Construction</u>
     <u>and Development of a Basketball Skill Test</u>. 1978. 14 p.
     (ERIC ED 190 514).

     Lists resources pertaining to the construction and development of a
     basketball skill test as a reflection of basketball playing ability.

55. <u>National Wheelchair Basketball Association - Directory</u>. Ed. by
     Stan Labanowich. Lexington, KY: National Wheelchair Basketball
     Association. Annual. 19? -   .

     Arranged by name of conference, 315 officers, team representatives,
     and game officials for each conference in the NWBA are covered.
     Entries include name, address, team name, and phone number for
     team representatives. (Based on 1980 secondary source.)

4.
BOATING SPORTS

In selecting sources to be included in this section, primary con-
sideration was given to those whose content focused at least in part on
the Olympic sports of yachting, canoeing, kayaking, and rowing. Motor
boating is represented only in those sources that cover a variety of
boating sports.

CATALOGS

56. BUC New Boat Price Guide. Ft. Lauderdale, FL: BUC International.
    Annual. 1963?-   . illus. index.

    This guide lists manufacturers' prices by model number/name. To
    aid the prospective boat buyer, such additional information as hull
    material, top or rig options, and engine types are included. This
    title was formerly called BUC's Boating Guide and BUC's New Boating
    Directory. Two indexes: one for boat manufacturer and one for
    engine manufacturer. (1981 ed. examined.)

57. BUC Older Boat Price Guide: 1905-1968 Models including Antiques
    and Classics. Ft. Lauderdale, FL: BUC International, 1980.
    256 p. index.

    This source uses actual used boat sales prices reported by dealers,
    brokers and surveyors to arrive at the current retail prices of
    over 70,000 used pleasure boats from 1905-1968. To help the user
    arrive at a more current assessment of a particular boat's current
    market value, the guide has two separate scales as supplements to
    its listed retail prices: one for geographical area and one for
    condition and equipment. (Based on 1980 secondary source.)

58. BUC Used Boat Price Guide. Ft. Lauderdale, FL: BUC International.
    Semi-annual. 1961?-   . index.

    Part of the BUC series, this title acts as a "Blue Book" of current
    market prices for used boats. It has undergone numerous title
    changes and is now published semi-annually in April and October.
    (Based on 1980 secondary source.)

59. The Mariner's Catalog: A Book of Information for Those Concerned
     with Boats and the Sea. Camden, ME: International Marine Pub.
     Annual. 1973-   . index. ISSN 0198-9618.

     A nautical "Whole Earth Catalog" which adds a new volume annually.
     Sources of information are varied, and include manufacturers' ad-
     dresses, photographs, and diagrams, all interspersed with comments,
     testimonials, and evaluations of items mentioned. (1973-78 eds.
     examined.)

60. Stearns, William, and Fern Stearns. The Canoeist's Catalog. Cam-
     den, ME: International Marine Pub., 1978. 191 p. illus. index.
     LC 77-85405.

     A very readable catalog arranged by such topics as canoe accesso-
     ries, canoeing handbooks, conservation, etc. Within each, the au-
     thors adopt a conversational style in discussing books, manufac-
     turers' catalogs, and the like. Names and addresses appear in
     bold type for easy identification.

61. Annual Yacht Survey Reports. Washington, DC: Independent Yacht
     Survey Co. Annual. 1978-   . illus.

     Although not technically a catalog, this survey evaluates yachts --
     a sort of "Consumer's Report" for yacht buyers. Each yacht sur-
     veyed merits a page of text and a facing page illustrating the mo-
     del. Each model is evaluated on design, performance, materials and
     workmanship, engines, rigging, etc. (Based on 1980 secondary source.)

DICTIONARIES

62. Biron, Pierre. Lexique Nautique: Anglais - Francais. Montreal,
     QUE: Pierre Biron, 1981. 194 p. (SIRC GV 775 #11427).

     In dictionary format, lists English nautical terms with French
     equivalents.

63. Blackburn, Graham. The Overlook Illustrated Dictionary of Nautical
     Terms. Woodstock, NY: Overlook Press, 1981. 349 p. illus.
     LC 80-39640.

     About 2,500 nautical terms concisely defined. Omitted are names
     of people, specific ships, types of vessels, and events. Emphasis
     is on terms relating to sailing. Numerous line drawings supple-
     ment entries.

64. Bradford, Graham. The Mariner's Dictionary. Barre, MA: Barre
     Publishers, 1972. 307 p. illus. LC 72-77971.

     Brings together terms with which a seaman should be familiar. The
     first edition, published in 1927, was entitled The Glossary of Sea
     Terms, and the author's lively preface states that he compiled the
     dictionary as he heard seamen use the terms. Vocabulary relates
     to the parts of a vessel, different types of craft, and various
     maneuvers.

65. Burgess, F. H. A Dictionary for Yachtsmen. North Pomfret, VT:
     David and Charles, 1981. 256 p. illus. LC 80-85494.

     Brief, concise definitions of terms and phrases commonly used by
     seamen. Also includes such items as the Flags of the International
     Code of Signals, semaphore code positions, illustrations of differ-
     ent types of buoys, etc. (1974 ed. examined.)

66. Clarkson, Henry. The Yachtsman's A to Z. New York: Arco, 1979.
     160 p. illus. LC 77-29252.

     Designed for the novice, this dictionary illustrates most of the
     terms it defines. It is not definitive, but as a reference tool it
     has great value in helping someone understand an unfamiliar term or
     concept. For example, the dictionary shows how to do herring-bone
     stitching, how to mouse a hook (lashing to prevent unhooking), etc.

67. Noel, John V. The Boating Dictionary: Sail and Power. New York:
     Van Nostrand Reinhold, 1981. 295 p. LC 80-19804.

     An alphabetical list of terms which includes acronyms (LORAN), ini-
     tialisms (PHRF), and names of individual boat models and their manu-
     facturer.

68. Rousmaniere, John. A Glossary of Modern Sailing Terms. New York:
     Dodd, Mead, 1976. 144 p. illus. LC 75-31504.

     An up-to-date guide to terminology in current use through the mid
     1970's. For completeness, see Bradford's The Mariner's Dictionary
     (#64). Definitions are generally brief, with occasional illustra-
     tions.

69. Shuwall, Melissa. Running Press Glossary of Sailing Language. Phi-
     ladelphia, PA: Running Press, 1977. 88 p. illus. LC 77-639.

     A glossary of 1000 terms and jargon pertaining to sailing and nau-
     tical navigation for lay people and professionals.

DIRECTORIES AND LOCATIONAL SOURCES

70. Makens, James C. Canoe Trails Directory. Garden City, NY: Double-
     day, 1979. 360 p. bibl. LC 76-42426.

     Updates the 1971 ed. Arranged alphabetically by state. Each trail
     is described and rated for difficulty. Alphabetical trails index
     at front. Suggested readings arranged by state.

71. Pyle, Sara. Canoeing and Rafting: The Complete Where-To-Go Guide
     to America's Best Tame and Wild Waters. New York: Morrow, 1979.
     363 p. LC 78-26272.

     A state-by-state directory of canoeing waters. Includes names, ad-
     dresses, and phone numbers of places to write for information on
     both canoeing and camping.

ENCYCLOPEDIAS

72. Encyclopedia of Sailing. Rev. and updated by the eds. of Yacht
     Racing/Cruising, with Robert Scharff and Richard Henderson. New
     York: Harper and Row, 1978. 468 p. illus. LC 76-26233.

     Organized by topic, this encyclopedia relies on a detailed table of
     contents to substitute for an index. It includes a catalog of sail-
     boats and two sections on racing and sailing competitions. A brief
     glossary of sailing terms follows the text.

73. Lucas, Alan. The Illustrated Encyclopedia of Boating. New York:
     Scribner's, 1977. 272 p. illus. LC 78-9809.

     Lavishly illustrated dictionary of yachting which includes sketches
     and photographs to explain particular terms. Every possible piece
     of a yacht is labeled in some fashion throughout the book.

74. Richey, Michael, ed. The Sailing Encyclopedia. New York: Lippin-
     cott and Crowell, 1980. 288 p. illus. LC 79-3821.

     An A-Z format which mixes short definitions with lengthy discussions
     of terms and concepts. Many of the articles include glossaries at
     the end of the text, e.g., a 13-page entry on "masts and rigging"
     has a glossary on the last two pages. Full page photographs en-
     hance the work, and "see" references abound.

75. Visual Encyclopedia of Nautical Terms Under Sail. New York: Crown,
     1978. (Various paging). illus. bibl. index. LC 77-28560.

     Terms are arranged alphabetically within subject categories (e.g.
     Sailors' Life, Customs and Tools), with an index in the back to tie
     it all together. The illustrations are excellent and include color/
     black and white photographs, drawings, cartoons, and paintings.

OTHER

76. Bottomley, Tom, ed. Boatman's Handbook: The New Look-It-Up Book.
     New York: Motor Boating and Sailing Books, 1975. 308 p. illus.
     LC 76-172013.

     Organized by sections like "Government Requirements", "Boat Racing",
     "Maintenance", and "Useful Tables", this book uses a system of black
     arrows keyed to edges. No index. To be useful, this book needs
     regular updating.

77. Piloting Seamanship and Small Boat Handling. By Charles F. Chapman.
     New York: Motor Boating and Sailing Book Division of Hearst
     Books. Annual. 1942-   . illus. index.

Published annually since 1942, this source has become a standard. It contains information on nautical terms, laws and regulations, rules of the road, seamanship, yachting etiquette, etc. and is replete with illustrations, diagrams, tables, and charts. (1978 ed. examined.)

78. Johnson, Peter. Boating Facts and Feats. New York: Sterling, 1979. 256 p. illus. index. LC 76-1163.

This is one of the Guinness Family of Books series. Records are arranged by categories (e.g. speed, size, endurance, unusual cruising exploits). Well illustrated. Indexed by name, subject, and boat in one alphabetical arrangement.

79. NAAO Rowing Guide. Philadelphia, PA: National Association of American Oarsmen. Annual. 1975-   .

Designed in 5 x 7, 6 ring format and bound with twine, pages can be replaced as necessary. Includes the constitution, bylaws and officials of the NAAO, laws of boat racing, regatta rules, Olympic rowing records, and various other competition winners and schools that participate in rowing. Formerly called Official Rowing Guide. (1975 ed. examined.)

80. North American Yacht Register. New York: Livingstone Marine Services. Annual. 1903-   . index. ISSN 0076-0226.

This source continues Lloyd's Register of American Yachts 1903-1977, and covers about 8,000 yacht and flag owners who have paid for a listing. Entries include yacht name, owner, descriptive information, home port, and port of registration. (1980 ed. examined.)

81. Rigg, H. K. Rigg's Handbook of Nautical Etiquette. New York: Alfred A. Knopf, 1971. 126 p. illus. index. LC 74-127089.

The tradition of yachting brings with it many customs and points of protocol. Some of these are just common sense, e.g., it is rude to peer through other crafts' portholes or cabin windows while docked in a marina, while others deal with such topics as sea burials and the naming of a yacht.

5.
BOWLING

82. <u>Bowling and Billiard Buyers Guide</u>. Chicago, IL: National Bowlers
    Journal, Inc. Annual. 19?-   . index.

    Published with, but separate from, <u>National Bowlers Journal and
    Billiard Review</u>. Covers about 500 manufacturers and suppliers of
    bowling equipment and their distributors. Product index. (Based
    on 1980 secondary source.)

83. Liss, Howard. <u>Bowling Talk for Beginners</u>. New York: J. Messner,
    1973. 80 p. illus. LC 72-11883.

    Although geared for young adults, this source does clearly explain
    the jargon used by bowlers. Only useful for novices.

6.
BOXING

BIOGRAPHICAL SOURCES

84. Burrill, Bob. Who's Who in Boxing. New Rochelle, NY: Arlington House, 1974. 208 p. LC 73-13020.

Alphabetically arranged are brief biographical sketches of over 400 boxers, managers, promoters, and others associated with boxing. International coverage from the late nineteenth century to early 1970's. Some discrepancies and omissions.

85. Heller, Peter. In This Corner; Forty World Champions Tell Their Stories. New York: Simon and Schuster, 1973. 432 p. illus. index. LC 73-8227.

Based on transcripts of interviews with 40 world champions, this work is arranged chronologically by decade, starting with the 1912-1919 period through the sixties, and then chronologically by the date the boxer became a world champion. Articles average between 10 to 15 pages, with personal and career information preceding each transcript.

86. Houston, Graham. Superfists. New York: Bounty Books, 1975. 176 p. illus. LC 75-13824.

Two to three pages of biographical information interspersed with black and white photographs for 27 "universally-accepted" heavyweight champions. Fight records conclude this work.

87 McCallum, John D. The Encyclopedia of World Boxing Champions Since 1882. Radnor, PA: Chilton, 1975. 337 p. illus. index. LC 75-19012.

Arranged by the eight categories of boxers (heavyweight, light heavyweight, etc.) and then chronologically according to each man's place on the list of champions, this is a collection of sketches of both the careers and personalities of boxing champions. Entries vary in length from a few lines to several pages, with American boxers generally having longer entries. Appendixes list members of the Hall of Fame, dates of title fights, fight records of all champions, and principal rules.

88. Weston, Stanley. The Heavyweight Champions. New York: Ace Books,
       1976. 337 p. illus. LC 76-150200.

     Nine to fifteen page biographies of 25 all-time, heavyweight cham-
     pions.

DICTIONARIES

89. Avis, Frederick C. Boxing Reference Dictionary. New York: Philo-
       sophical Library, 1958. 127 p. LC 58-3356.

     Defines major terms in boxing, standard championship weights, the
     jargon of the ring, many of the nicknames of famous boxers and
     knuckle-fighters, training hints and equipment, and many other
     items of boxing information.

90. Eduardo-Gonzalez, C. F. Boxing Fan's Glossary. n.p. Eduardo-Gon-
       zalez, 1980. 47 p. LC 80-65019.

     An author-published dictionary containing rather superficial defi-
     nitions of boxing fans' terminology. Unique, however, in its pur-
     pose and audience.

STATISTICAL SOURCES

91. The Ring Record Book and Boxing Encyclopedia. Ed. by B. Sugar and
       staff of Ring Magazine. New York: Atheneum. Annual. 1942-

     Begun by Nat Fleischer in 1941 and published annually, this "bible
     of boxing" provides career data and comprehensive records for box-
     ers from many countries from 1719 to the present. 1981 edition has
     directory of managers and a name index. (1981 ed. examined.)

7.
CRICKET

BIBLIOGRAPHICAL SOURCES

92. Padwick, E. W., comp. A Bibliography of Cricket. London, ENG: The Library Association, 1977. 649 p. illus. index. LC 77-367689.

A comprehensive list of over 8,000 titles of books, pamphlets, brochures, yearbooks and periodicals published in early 19th century up to 1973. Includes foreign publications from countries of the Commonwealth. Titles are grouped by "General Works", "Cricket in Different Countries", "International Cricket", "Literature, Games, Biography, Records". Alphabetical index of titles and names.

93. Taylor, Alfred D. The Catalogue of Cricket Literature. Wakefield, ENG: S. R. Publishers, 1972. 115 p. LC 73-157596.

Reprint of 1906 edition which lists books and periodicals with UK imprints. Arrangement is alphabetical by authors and titles. Annotations include the market value of the rarer books. The earliest one listed was published in 1799.

BIOGRAPHICAL SOURCES

94. Batchelor, Denzil, ed. Great Cricketers. London, ENG: Eyre & Spottiswoode, 1970. 368 p. illus. index. LC 71-529352.

Reprints of biographies written between 1929 to 1970 from more than 20 cricket magazines and books. Of the 63 cricketers included are Australian, Indian, Pakistan, and West Indies players. Index of authors.

95. Frith, David, ed. Cricket Gallery: Fifty Profiles of Famous Players From "The Cricketer". Guildford, ENG: Lutterworth Press, 1976. 256 p. illus. index. LC 77-354241.

A collection of 50 profiles of famous players from the "gallery" column of a monthly magazine The Cricketer between 1970 and 1976. An update of each is given as footnotes to the original articles. Includes players from England, Australia, West Indies, New Zealand, India, and Pakistan.

96.   Frith, David. The Fast Men: A 200-year Cavalcade of Speed Bowlers. Rev. and updated ed. London, ENG: Corgi Books, 1977. 221 p. illus. bibl. index. LC 77-378029.

A collection of anecdotes, facts, and figures of international speed giants. This book records the achievements of players by tracing their careers in groups of 4 to 6. Players index.

97.   Lyttelton, R. H., W. J. Ford, C. B. Fry and G. Giffen. Giants of the Game: Being Reminiscences of the Stars of Cricket from Daft Down to 1900. Wakefield, ENG: E. P. Publishing, 1973. 192 p. illus. LC 74-188118.

A reprint of 1899 publication. As stated in the introduction, it is a "series of expert assessments of outstanding players by four knowledgeable cricketers..." Also included are Australian players. No index.

98.   Martin-Jenkins, Christopher. The Complete Who's Who of Test Cricketers. London, ENG: Orbis Publishing, 1980. 424 p. illus. LC 80-512421.

Concise biographies of test cricketers, grouped by countries, beginning with the British, followed by the Australian, etc. No index. Table of contents lists the countries in paging sequence. Includes deceased players.

DICTIONARIES/ENCYCLOPEDIAS

99.   Golesworthy, Maurice. Encyclopaedia of Cricket. 6th ed. London, ENG: R. Hale, 1977. 222 p. illus. bibl. index. LC 77-362672.

This source has biographical information on famous players through the 1976 season. Also lengthy descriptions of major clubs in different countries.

100. Swanton, E. W., OBE, gen. ed. Barclays World of Cricket -- The Game from A to Z. New ed. London, ENG: Collins, in association with Barclays Bank Int., 1980. 662 p. illus. index. LC 80-148067.

Comprehensive treatment of the history of cricket, biographies, glossary, treasury (arts, books, broadcasting, etc.), cricket grounds of the world, and statistics up to end of 1979 English season. Single index of persons, places, teams, events, etc.

STATISTICAL SOURCES

101. Dalby, Ken. Headingley Test Cricket 1899-1975. Otley, ENG:
      Olicana Books Ltd., 1976. 158 p. illus. LC 76-376880.

      Statistics and descriptive notes on Headingley Test matches chrono-
      logically arranged in chapters from 1899 through 1975.

102. Gibb, James, comp. Test Cricket Records from 1877. Glasgow, SCOT:
      Collins, 1979. 210 p. LC 80-467195.

      Statistics on test cricket.

103. Green, Benny, ed. Wisden Anthology 1864-1900. London, ENG: Mac-
      donald and Jane's, 1979. 975 p. index.

      Expanded and updated edition of the Wisden's Almanack (#104). De-
      scriptive and statistical data on country matches and foreign
      teams, with obituaries and notable feats.

104. Wisden Cricketers' Almanack. London, ENG: Sporting Handbooks
      Ltd. Annual. 1864-1978.

      A standard, important annual of the cricket world, with comprehen-
      sive cricket records by teams, by cup, and by matches, including
      public schools and foreign countries. Other features are cricket-
      ers of the year, obituary and articles on world champion team, and
      laws of cricket. (115th ed. 1978 examined.)

8.
CURLING

105. Maxwell, Doug, et al. <u>The First Fifty -- A Nostalgic Look at the Brier</u>. Toronto, ONT: Douglas D. Maxwell Ltd., 1980. 120 p. illus. LC 80-512267.

Encyclopedic treatment of history of curling from its beginning in 1927 to the present. Year by year round-up of champions and records, all-time team records, individual highlights, trophy winners, and curling Hall of Fame members.

106. Thiessen, Roy D. <u>Curling Handbook for Curlers, Teachers, and Coaches</u>. Saanichton, BC: Hancock House, 1977. 88 p. illus. bibl. LC 77-2578.

Of borderline reference value, this is basically a handbook on the "how" of training and play. The chapters on terminology and equipment enhance its reference value.

9.
CYCLING

BIBLIOGRAPHICAL SOURCES

107. Luebbers, David J. The Bicycle Resource Guide. Denver, CO:
Silers Print Co. Irreg. 1978-   . index. ISSN 0193-8584.

This source continues the non-cumulative series, formerly called
Bicycle Bibliography (ISSN 0098-1230), of which there are 5 issues
published between 1972 and 1977. In most all these issues, books,
periodical articles, and some documents and newspaper articles are
listed and annotated in publication type categories. All aspects
of cycling covered. Multiple indexes. Since 1978 two issues of
the current title have been published: The 1978 Bicycle Resources
Guide (1978) and the 1981 Bicycle Resources Guide (1981). The 1981
Guide is organized by publication type, citing and annotating 2,078
items on all aspects of cycling. Articles from 11 newspapers are
listed in the newspaper section. Author, corporate, geographical,
and subject indexes. (1981 ed. examined.)

108. Schultz, Barbara A., and Mark P. Schultz. Bicycles and Bicycling:
A Guide to Information Sources. Sports, Games, and Pastimes Information Guide Series, Vol. 6. Detroit, MI: Gale, 1979. 300 p.
index. LC 79-22839.

Extremely thorough guide with sections on general sources, history,
technique, competition, touring, transportation, design and construction, maintenance and repair, legal aspects, and statistics.
Among the resources included are organization, manufacturers and
suppliers, books, periodicals, U.S. government publications, au-
diovisuals, and seminars, conferences, and workshops.

109. Swim, Frances F., comp. Bicycling and Bicycle Trails. Washington,
DC: Dept. of the Interior, Office of Library Service, 1971.
29 p. index. (SUDOC I22.7/2:24).

Scope includes most all aspects of bicycles and bicycling, although
recreational aspects are predominant. Includes books, periodical
articles, and technical reports published between 1920-1970. Brief
annotations. Subject index.

DIRECTORIES AND LOCATIONAL SOURCES

110. Bicycle Dealer Showcase -- Buyer's Guide Issue. Ed. by Steve
     Ready. Santa Ana, CA: William Lawrence Co. Annual. 19?-
     index.

     Geographical arrangement of about 2,000 manufacturers, wholesalers,
     and distributers of bicycles and mopeds. Address, phone, and sales
     contact provided for each. Brand and trade name indexes. (Based
     on 1980 secondary source.)

111. Browder, Sue. American Biking Atlas and Touring Guide. New York:
     Workman Publishing Co., 1974. 320 p. illus. maps. LC 75-8816.

     Detailed explanations and maps for 150 tours in U.S. and Canada.
     Index of tours at end.

112. Gilbert, Dave, ed. The American Bicycle Atlas. New York: E. P.
     Dutton, 1981. 271 p. maps. LC 80-68799.

     Produced by American Youth Hostels, this source is both a guide-
     book to 96 bicycle routes in the U.S. and a guide to equipment
     selection, bicycle repair, and safety. Also, a directory of bi-
     cycle organizations and AYH councils are included along with sour-
     ces of maps.

113. Green, Susan, comp. Cyclists' Yellow Pages: A Complete Resource
     Guide to Maps, Books, Routes, Organizations, and Group Tours.
     Rev. ed. Missoula, MT: Bikecentennial, 1980. 62 p.

     A handy resource listing cycling organizations, directory of or-
     ganizational sources for maps (U.S. and Canada), and brief list of
     cycling books and periodicals. Updates their Resource Directory
     for Bicycle Tourists (1976). Recreational focus.

OTHER

114. Heilman, Gail, ed. The Complete Outfitting and Source Book for
     Bicycle Touring. Marshall, CA: Great Outdoors Trading Co.;
     distr. New York: Holt, Rinehart and Winston, 1980. 256 p.
     illus. maps. LC 79-55215.

     General coverage of such touring topics as: equipment, accessor-
     ies, history, publications, clubs, organizations, touring routes
     in the U.S. and Canada, etc. Sources of further information are
     provided for touring routes and maps and package tours. Appen-
     dixes include an equipment/supplies checklist, custom frame build-
     ers, and addresses of equipment manufacturers. Two page glossary
     completes this source.

115. <u>International Cycling Guide</u>. Ed. by Nicholas Crane. So. Bruns-
        wick, NJ: A. S. Barnes. Annual. 1980-   . illus.

      A thorough source of international information on cycling. Arti-
      cles on bikes of the year, racing events of the year, fitness and
      safety, bicycle planning research, new equipment, and cycle shows
      are combined with a directory of international cycling organiza-
      tions, an annotated list of current cycling books, and an inter-
      national list of dealers. (1980 ed. examined.)

10.
EQUESTRIAN SPORTS

Because there are so many reference works dealing with horses, horsemanship, and equestrian sports, selection for this section required that at least a fairly substantive part of the book be devoted to any of the equestrian events in the Olympic Games or other competitive, spectator equestrian sports. Therefore, reference works dealing primarily with other recreational (e.g., horse camping) or commercial aspects of horses (e.g., breeding) are excluded. Admittedly, excellent non-North American and pre-1970 imprints are available for these sports, and the reader is encouraged to consult the major bibliographies listed, #117 and #118.

BIBLIOGRAPHICAL SOURCES

116. Pady, Donald S. Horses and Horsemanship: Selected Books and Periodicals in the Iowa State University Library: An Annotated Bibliography. Ames, IO: Iowa State University Library, 1973. 226 p. illus. index.

Arranged by broad subject sections, this annotated bibliography includes nearly 800 titles for books and periodicals published as early as 1475 through 1972 held by the Univ. of Iowa Library. Author/title indexes.

117. Smith, Myron J. Equestrian Studies: The Salem College Guide to Sources in English, 1950-1980. Metuchen, NJ: Scarecrow Press, 1981. 361 p. index. LC 81-2002.

A nearly comprehensive classified bibliography of English-language books, periodical articles and 16 mm films on all aspects of horses and horsemanship. Author index only.

118. Wells, Ellen B. Horsemanship: A Guide to Information Sources. Sports, Games and Pastimes Information Guide Series, no. 4. Detroit, MI: Gale, 1979. 138 p. index. LC 79-16046.

This annotated guide to the literature is arranged in two parts:
the first includes sections on organizations, periodicals, audio-
visuals, museums and libraries; the second is a selective, annotated bibliography of standard references as well as more recent
titles covering all aspects of horsemanship, horses, equipment, and
equestrian sports. Many foreign publications are included. Au-
thor/title/subject index.

BIOGRAPHICAL SOURCES

119.   Drager, Marvin. The Most Glorious Crown. New York: Winchester
       Press, 1975. 216 p. illus. bibl. index. LC 74-16864.

A unique source for both reference and general collections, that
details the stories of nine horses who have won the elusive Triple
Crown. From Sir Barton in 1919 to Secretariat in 1973, the racing
and stud careers of these horses are portrayed. In addition, other
great horses of the time are alluded to. An appendix includes miscellaneous statistics, a glossary and a bibliography.

120.   Fetros, John G. Dictionary of Factual and Fictional Horses and
       their Riders. Hicksville, NY: Exposition Press, 1979. 200 p.
       bibl. index. LC 79-51665.

Alphabetically arranged by the name of the individual associated
with the horse, the entries describe famous and notorious horses
and their owners in history and legend. Appendix lists the persons
and their horses included in the book. A separate index of horses
is a cross-reference to the main entries.

DICTIONARIES

121.   Devlin, C. B. Horseman's Dictionary: Medical and General. South
       Brunswick, NJ: A. S. Barnes, 1974. 134 p. illus. LC 73-10518.

Defines the anatomical, physiological, medical, and some race horse
terminology. Well illustrated. Stable jargon defined in a separate
section.

122.   Stratton, Charles. The International Horseman's Dictionary. New
       York: Dial, 1975. 256 p. illus. LC 75-8650.

Generously illustrated, this very comprehensive dictionary includes
items for horses, equipment, horse racing, important personalities
of equestrian world, hunting, dressage and polo. A 30-page section lists winners for a variety of international equestrian competitions, including the Olympic Games.

123.   Van Tuyl, Barbara. The Horseman's Book. Englewood Cliffs, NJ:
       Prentice-Hall, 1973. 262 p. illus. LC 73-9739.

Written for the novice, this glossary covers thoroughbred racing, harness racing, shows, foxhunting, dressage, polo, breeding, and equipment.

DIRECTORIES AND LOCATIONAL SOURCES

124. Directory and Record Book. Lake Success, NY: Thoroughbred Racing Assns. Annual. 1955-   . illus. ISSN 0082-4240.

Arranged geographically, this annual is a compendium of information on racetracks in U.S. and Canada, yearly records, racing dates, and listings of awards for various racing world competitions. 1980 ed. also provides information about the TRA and its services, the Triple Crown, and the National Racing Hall of Fame. Description of each track is quite detailed. (1980 ed. examined.)

125. Dressage Directory: Instructors, Clinicians, and Officials. Lincoln, NE: U.S. Dressage Federation. Annual. 1973-   .

Provides names, addresses, phone numbers and occupational specialization of about 500 dressage instructors and clinicians at all levels, American Horse Shows Assoc. licensed dressage judges, and technical delegates. Arranged geographically with personal name and occupation indexes. (Formerly titled Directory of Dressage Instructors.) (Based on 1980 secondary source.)

126. Norback, Craig T. The Horseman's Catalog. New York: McGraw-Hill, 1979. 520 p. illus. LC 79-14307.

Much more than a simple directory, this source provides brief articles and names and locations for more information for all aspects of the horse industry. Of interest for equestrian sports are: the listings of dressage instructors, breed registries, equine publications, horse museums, halls of fame and libraries, associations, and racing tracks.

127. Spector, David A. A Guide to American Horse Shows. New York: Arco, 1973. 128 p. illus. LC 72-86239.

A chronological guide to 50 of the major horse shows in the U.S. and Canada. Keyed to the hunter-jumper exhibitor, the guide emphasizes shows in the East. History and background of each show are given, as are data on types of classes offered, ratings, dates and place held, etc.

128. The Thoroughbred Owners and Breeders Directory. Lexington, KY: Thoroughbred Owners and Breeders Assn. Annual. 1976-   . ISSN 0364-7137.

Annual publication listing names and addresses of U.S. owners and breeders of thoroughbreds. (1981 ed. examined.)

129. U. S. Dressage Federation Calendar of Competitions. Lincoln, NE:
      U. S. Dressage Federation. Semiannual. 19?-   .

      Arranged geographically, this source covers about 150 dressage com-
      petitions. Entries provide competition name, date, location, le-
      vels of training included in competition, and name, address, and
      phone of contact. (Based on 1980 secondary source.)

ENCYCLOPEDIAS

130. Ainslie, Tom. Ainslie's Encyclopedia of Thoroughbred Handicapping.
      New York: William Morrow, 1978. 320 p. index. LC 78-9755.

      Alphabetically arranged entries of varying length (some are 2 - 3
      pages), this encyclopedia approaches comprehensiveness for this
      subject. Much of this information has been presented in Ainslie's
      other books on handicapping, but not in an encyclopedia format.
      Wealth of detail about thoroughbred racing, tracks and their man-
      agements, and the theory and practice of handicapping. Glossary
      and index.

131. Churchill, Peter. Riding from A to Z: A Practical Manual of Horse-
      manship. New York: Taplinger Pub., 1978. 152 p. illus. index.
      LC 77-88451.

      This source's scope covers all aspects of training riders, including
      sections on the history of equitation, clothing, equipment, jumping,
      purchase and care of a horse, competition riding, and a career with
      horses. Effective illustrations.

132. Clayton, Michael, and William Steinkraus, eds. The Complete Book
      of Show Jumping. New York: Crown, 1975. 264 p. illus. bibl.
      index. LC 74-24775.

      Even with its British perspective this source treats show jumping
      as an international style. Not a how-to book, major sections in-
      clude show jumping in Europe and North American and selection, train-
      ing and care. About half of the book is devoted to descriptions of
      leading riders and horses.

133. Edwards, Elwyn H., ed. Encyclopedia of the Horse. New York:
      Crescent Books, 1980. 256 p. illus. index. LC 80-7680.

      Profusely illustrated (mostly color), the signed articles are ar-
      ranged in four broad categories: development of the horse, eques-
      trian sports, breeds, and horse care and management. Especially
      good, lengthy articles on dressage, show jumping and the three-day
      event. A glossary of equestrian terms and an index complete this
      source.

134. Herbert, Ivor, ed. Horse Racing: The Complete Guide to the World
      of the Turf. New York: St. Martins, 1981. 256 p. illus. in-
      dex. LC 81-47018.

Organized in 4 major sections -- "Story of Racing," "World of
Racing," "Great Courses," and "Great Horses of the Past" -- authoritative, international coverage is provided. For 13 countries, detailed information, illustrations, and a location map are provided
for the major race courses. Brief biographical and career information is provided for notable contemporary owners, trainers, jockeys,
and famous horses from the last 25 years. A statistical glossary,
giving the most important racing records and other statistics of
the last 25 years completes this comprehensive source.

135. Hope, Charles E., and G. N. Jackson, eds. The Encyclopedia of the
      Horse. New York: Viking, 1973. 336 p. illus. LC 72-90351.

An authoritative, international encyclopedia on all facets of horses, breeds, and equestrian sports. All entries signed; longer articles have a brief list of references for further reading.

136. Kidd, Jane, et. al., comp. The Complete Horse Encyclopedia. New
      York: Chartwell Books, 1976. 256 p. illus. bibl. index.
      LC 76-22860.

First half of book deals with breeds, health and training of horses,
while second half is devoted to the competitive aspects of the
sport. Includes various types of racing, and contains a section on
dressage, vaulting, polo, etc. Appendices include information on
pony clubs, equestrian organizations, and a short bibliography.

137. Ljungquist, Bengt. Practical Dressage Manual. 2nd ed. Richmond,
      VA: Whittet and Shepperson, 1977. 166 p. illus. index. LC
      76-15459.

Although not strictly a reference book, this manual comprehensively
covers all aspects of competitive dressage. Most of the definitions
used are taken from the Federation Equestre Internationale Rulebook
and the AHSA Notes on Dressage. Illustrations and diagrams are
plentiful.

138. Pines, Philip A. The Complete Book of Harness Racing. 3rd ed.
      New York: Arco, 1978. 331 p. illus. index. LC 77-722.

A comprehensive survey of harness racing from its beginning to early
1970's. Includes profiles of famous horses, drivers, and trainers;
. a glossary of terms; and sections on equipment, training methods,
betting, and handicapping. Many illustrations and an appendix of
selected racing records and statistics complement this source.

139. Skelton, Betty. Rand McNally Pictorial Encyclopedia of Horses and
      Riding. Chicago, IL: Rand McNally, 1978. 216 p. illus. index.
      LC 77-82259.

Although over half the book is devoted to breeds, the care and
training of horses, and riding skills, two sections include articles on competitive equestrian activities. Category arrangement.
Brief glossary.

140. Summerhays, Reginald S., comp. Revised by Stella Walker. Sum-
     merhays' Encyclopedia for Horsemen. 6th rev. ed. New York: F.
     Warne, 1975. 419 p. illus. LC 79-114792.

     Although prior editions reflected a heavily British emphasis, this
     6th rev. ed. has broadened its scope to include more articles on
     international equestrian activities. In one alphabetical arrange-
     ment signed, lengthy articles written by contemporary experts are
     interfiled with brief entries. Results of championship competi-
     tions, horse races, etc. are in a final section.

141. Taylor, Louis. Harper's Encyclopedia for Horsemen: The Complete
     Book of the Horse. New York: Harper & Row, 1973. 558 p. il-
     lus. bibl. LC 72-79697.

     Most all aspects of horsemanship, horses, and equestrian sports in-
     cluded. Entries range from one paragraph to three to four pages.

STATISTICAL SOURCES

142. American Racing Manual. Chicago, IL: Daily Racing Form. Annual.
     1906-   . illus. index.

     Published each summer, this source tabulates and reviews the events
     of the previous year and updates essential long-term statistics.
     Contents include the record of every active horse, owner, trainer,
     and rider; results charts of the most lucrative stakes; some his-
     torical material; descriptions of noteworthy accomplishments of
     horses and persons; and presents diagrams and measurements of all
     tracks. (1979 ed. examined.)

143. Annual Yearbook of Trotting and Pacing. Columbus, OH: U.S. Trot-
     ting Association. Annual. 1939-   . ISSN 0083-3517.

     Contains statistical information, world records, summaries of race
     meetings in U.S. and Canada during previous year, alphabetical list
     of all horses, their breeding, earnings, etc. (Based on 1980 se-
     condary source.)

11.
FENCING

144. Manley, Albert. Complete Fencing. Garden City, NY: Doubleday, 1979. 305 p. illus. bibl. index. LC 76-56319.

A manual on modern fencing for the student and coach, with separate chapters on foil, epee, and sabre. Illustrated descriptions are provided for technique, training and officiating. Its major reference value lies in the glossary and list of suppliers. Subject index.

145. National Intercollegiate Women's Fencing Association - Directory. Kearny, NJ: National Intercollegiate Women's Fencing Association. Annual. 19? - . index.

This "for members only" directory covers 70 colleges and universities with women's varsity fencing teams. Information includes institution's and team coach's names, address and phone. Alphabetical name index. (Based on 1980 secondary source.)

146. Thimm, Carl A. A Complete Bibliography of Fencing and Duelling. Bronx, NY: Benjamin Blom Inc., 1968. 537 p. illus. LC 68-17152.

A reprint of the 1896 edition, this bibliography is a monumental work that includes books, pamphlets, magazines, etc. published in all European languages since the Middle Ages. All accounts of duels are noted. Over 100 pages devoted to articles, speeches, and famous duels. Lots of portraits of leading masters. Subject index with entries in chronological order grouped by languages.

12.
FOOTBALL

Football has such a wealth of reference material that the reader is referred to Grobani's Guide to Football Literature (#147) for more comprehensive, although dated, citations. In this chapter we have tried to winnow out those titles likely to be most useful for general reference purposes. The appetite of sports fans for football statistics appears insatiable and has led to a proliferation of sources which we have grouped with statistics despite such titles as "guides," "handbooks," "digests," etc. We have also excluded those annuals for which no information could be obtained regarding current publishing activity.

BIBLIOGRAPHICAL SOURCES

147. Grobani, Anton. Guide to Football Literature. Detroit, MI: Gale, 1975. 319 p. illus. index. LC 75-1478.

Annotated bibliography of publications on amateur, high school, college and pro football in 33 categories, including individual team's press guides. Title index, and lack of appropriate subject access necessitates extensive browsing of main sections. Over 3000 entries.

148. Clemence, William J., and James Pitts. Annotated Football Bibliography. An Applied Project in Physical Education. Athens, GA: University of Georgia, 1977. 39 p. (ERIC ED 150 094).

This bibliography is limited to the areas of coaching techniques and philosophy, fundamentals, offense, defense, injuries and conditioning at the high school and college level. Materials available from the Univ. of Georgia libraries are heavily represented.

BIOGRAPHICAL SOURCES

149. Cohane, Tim. Great College Football Coaches of the Twenties and Thirties. New Rochelle, NY: Arlington House, 1973. 329 p. illus. index. LC 73-7543.

Profiles of 43 famous college coaches arranged in alphabetical order. Appendices provide their game-by-game records, and names of
other coaches.

150. Libby, Bill. Champions of College Football. New York: Hawthorn,
      1975. 205 p. illus. index. LC 74-31632.

A chronological history of college football which discusses the
players only in the context of a particular team or season. Statistical tables detail top teams, coaches, rankings, etc.

151. Mendell, Ronald L., and Timothy B. Phares. Who's Who in Football.
      New Rochelle, NY: Arlington House, 1974. 395 p. LC 74-17336.

Biographies of over 1400 football players, coaches, officials, etc.
of collegiate and professional teams. (Based on 1975 secondary
source.)

152. Schaap, Dick. Quarterbacks Have All the Fun. Chicago, IL: Play-
      boy Press, 1974. 260 p. illus. LC 74-82481.

Reprints of magazine articles on 19 quarterbacks written by various
editors, with an updated introduction for each by Schaap. Action
photos of eight players only.

153. Sullivan, George. The Gamemakers: Pro Football's Great Quarter-
      backs -- from Baugh to Namath. New York: G. P. Putnam's, 1971.
      illus. LC 76-163418.

Biographies of 17 famous pro quarterbacks which include accounts of
special games and plays -- career statistics follow each entry.

154. Sullivan, George. The Great Running Backs. New York: G. P. Put-
      nam's Sons, 1972. 253 p. illus. LC 72-79531.

Typical of similar biographical sources that are published about
playing positions, this source consists of 3 - 4 page profiles on
each of 32 running backs from 1900 to the '70's. Career rushing
record is included.

DICTIONARIES

155. Shefski, Bill. Running Press Glossary of Football Language. Phila-
      delphia, PA: Running Press, 1978. 120 p. LC 77-12492.

Definitions of jargon and slang used by reporting media such as TV
and newspaper reporters.

156. Sullivan, George. Pro Football A to Z: A Fully Illustrated Guide
      to America's Favorite Sport. New York: Winchester Press, 1975.
      341 p. illus. LC 75-9259.

Includes definitions, profiles of players, teams of various American and Canadian leagues, all members of Pro Football and Hall of
Fame.

ENCYCLOPEDIAS

157. Bennett, Tom, et al., eds. The NFL's Official Encyclopedic His-
      tory of Professional Football. 2nd ed. New York: Macmillan,
      1977. 512 p. illus. LC 76-30547.

      Based on the official records of the NFL, this is a standard source
      on the formation of the NFL, history of each team and annual team
      records. Different chapters on various games' records, biographies,
      rules. An interesting feature is information on pro football sta-
      diums, with diagrams and photos for each. No index.

158. Ecker, Tom, and Bill Calloway, eds. Athletic Journal's Encyclo-
      pedia of Football. West Nyack, NY: Parker Pub., 1978. 318 p.
      illus. LC 77-25127.

      Reprints of 49 articles by outstanding coaches, representing "the
      top thinking in the game today." The organization, by offense,
      defense, kicking game, etc., makes this a useful reference source.

159. McCallum, John, and Charles H. Pearson. College Football U.S.A.,
      1869-1972. Greenwich, CT: Hall of Fame Publishing Co., 1971.
      559 p. illus. LC 79-180212.

      Historical, biographical, and topical sketches (e.g., "Black foot-
      ball is beautiful," "Linger Oh Linger, Pudge Heffelfinger") are in-
      terspersed with such items as the evolution and digest of football
      rules, all time college football records, discussions of bowl games,
      roster of all-time, all-American teams, and summaries of the major
      teams from 1950 through 1970. Lack of an index hampers the book's
      overall usefulness.

160. Neft, David S., et al. Pro Football: The Early Years, an Ency-
      clopedic History, 1895-1959. Ridgefield, CT: Sports Products
      Inc., 1978. 288 p. LC 78-109096.

      The bulk of this book begins in 1920 with the founding of the Na-
      tional Football League, and is subsequently arranged by chronologi-
      cal periods. Statistics on games, teams, and players are given for
      each year thereafter. The series continues with Pro Football: The
      Modern Era from 1960, the advent of the American Football League,
      to the present.

161. Neft, David S., et al. The Sports Encyclopedia -- Pro Football:
      The Modern Era, 1960 to the Present. New York: Grosset & Dun-
      lap, 1978. 416 p. illus. LC 78-61243.

      A continuation of Pro Football: The Early Years. Arrangement is
      chronological, with statistics and text about teams, games, and
      players.

162. Treat, Roger L. The Encyclopedia of Football. 16th rev. ed. So.
      Brunswick, NJ: A. S. Barnes, 1979. 738 p. illus. LC 79-63272.

History of the game, year-by-year chronologies from 1919 to the
present, statistics and significant awards/records for players and
coaches, plus paid attendance figures and seating diagrams for several major stadiums. Also includes a history and information on ex-
tinct leagues. This source is revised every few years.

STATISTICAL SOURCES—COLLEGE

163. The Complete Handbook of College Football. Ed. by Zander Hollander.
      New York: New American Library. Annual. 1977-   . illus.
      ISSN 0149-0168.

      Forecasts of team performance based upon previous seasons' records.
      Arranged by conference within a geographic area. Listing is not
      as complete as title claims. (1977 ed. examined.)

164. Di Marco, Anthony. The Big Bowl Football Guide. Rev. ed. New
      York: G. P. Putnam's Sons, 1976. 152 p. illus. LC 76-8361.

      An "encyclopedia" of college bowl games with history, capsule sum-
      maries, and detailed year-by-year records from 1900 to 1976. Also
      includes all-star game scores. Profusely illustrated. No index.

165. NCAA Football. Shawnee Mission, KS: National Collegiate Athletic
      Association. Annual. 1889-   . illus.

      Beginning with a preview-review of the season, this guide provides
      analyses of teams by geographic regions, by division champions, and
      leading quarterbacks. Also includes statistics, records, and sche-
      dules. (Formerly known as the Official National Collegiate Athletic
      Association Football Guide.) (1980 ed. examined.)

166. NCAA Football Records. Shawnee Mission, KS: National Collegiate
      Athletic Association. Annual. 1969-   . ISSN 0092-881X.

      This compendium of college football statistics was formerly entitled
      College Football Modern Record Book. Includes both individual and
      team records, all-time statistical leaders, coaching records, win
      streaks, longest plays, and all-American teams since 1889. (Based
      on 1979 secondary source.)

167. Street & Smith's Official Yearbook: College Football. New York:
      Conde Nast. Annual. 1973-   . illus. ISSN 0091-9977.

      Team leaders, schedules, roster of players for college teams, pre-
      vious season's records, etc. (Based on 1979 secondary source.)

STATISTICAL SOURCES—PROFESSIONAL

168. Billings, Robert, ed. Pro Football Digest. Chicago, IL: Follett,
      1973. 288 p. illus. LC 73-83468.

A descriptive history of the greatest games, all pro-teams by de-
cades, etc., and statistical records of Super Bowl, championship
games, individual players, etc.

169. Canadian Football League's Official Record and Information Manual.
      Toronto, ONT: Canadian Football League. Annual. 1975-   .
      illus. ISSN 0708-6784.

      Formerly called CFL Official Yearbook (1973-1974), this source is
      jam-packed with such information as: history; listing of all pre-
      vious Grey Cup games; coaching records; records and highlights from
      the previous season; lists of all-star teams; major awards; members
      of the Hall of Fame; list of all-time records for the League; and
      addresses, officers, head coaches, stadiums, and colors for all the
      Canadian teams. (Based on 1979 secondary source.)

170. The Complete Handbook of Pro Football. Ed. by Zander Hollander.
      New York: New American Library. Annual. 1975-   . illus.
      ISSN 0361-2988.

      Contains feature articles of current interest, brief overviews of
      the strengths and weaknesses of each team in the AFL and the NFL,
      statistics, draft choices, standings and TV schedules. (1975 ed.
      examined.)

171. Football Register. St. Louis, MO: Sporting News. Annual. 1966-
           . ISSN 0071-7258.

      Alphabetically arranged by currently active players and coaches in
      the NFL, it provides complete season-by-season playing records, as
      well as players' birthdate, education, and other personal charac-
      teristics. (1980 ed. examined.)

172. National Football League -- Official Record Manual. New York: Na-
      tional Football League. Annual. 1947-   . illus. ISSN 0077-
      4588.

      A comprehensive compendium of records and statistics for each year's
      season. Some examples of data: American Football Conference and
      National Football Conference results, AFC, NFC, and NFL team sum-
      maries, individual statistics, etc. Players listed on the All-Pro
      team and Pro Hall of Fame are included. All-time records, and re-
      sults of the prior year's Super Bowl, Championship Games, AFC-NFC
      Pro Bowl, team directories and schedules are also found in this es-
      sential source. Official signals and helmet insignia are illus-
      trated. (1980 ed. examined.)

173. Official National Football League Guide. New York: New American
      Library. Annual. 1972-   . ISSN 0091-0821.

      Player statistics records, previews, rosters, photos. (Based on
      1975 secondary source.)

174. The Pocket Book of Pro Football. New York: Pocket Books. Annual.
      1963-   . illus. ISSN 0148-8007.

An attempt to size up the approaching season for each team in pro
football. Information includes previous year's record, schedule,
individual player statistics, diagrams of offensive and defensive
team starters, and discussions of each team's strengths and weaknesses. (1979 ed. examined.)

175. Pro Football. Los Angeles, CA: Peterson's Pub. Annual. 1960-
      . illus. index. ISSN 0079-5526.

Formerly titled Peterson's Pro Football Annual, this source includes articles, team directories, previous season's statistics,
predictions, NFL rule changes, roster of NFL game officials, and a
complete list of winners and losers of the Super Bowl. (Based on
1979 secondary source.)

176. Shapiro, David. The 135 Greatest Pro Running Backs: How They
      Stack Up Against Each Other. Berkeley, CA: SportsMinded Pub.,
      1978. 192 p. illus. LC 78-61360.

Designed to provide a yardstick to evaluate the relative proficiency
of professional running backs by putting into statistical perspec-
tive the year-to-year career records of 135 leading running backs,
active and retired. Part I has all the tables and final rankings
and Part II gives career records of individual players.

177. Sporting News' National Football Guide. St. Louis, MO: Sporting
      News. Annual. 1970-   . ISSN 0081-3788.

Very complete and authoritative, the strongest emphasis is on the
previous season and current team information for schedules, rules,
statistics, and players. Summarizes the previous season's games,
arranged chronologically, including description and box scores.
All-time records for NFL, AFL, and AAFC are also included. (Based
on 1979 secondary source.)

178. Street and Smith's Official Yearbook: Pro Football. New York:
      Conde Nast. Annual. 1972-   . illus. ISSN 0092-3214.

Includes draft information plus description of previous Super Bowl
and division championships. Separate articles on each team cover
leaders, schedules, previous season's scores, players, etc. NFC
and AFC previous season's records are also included. Provides
brief information on each team in the Canadian Football League.
(Based on 1979 secondary source.)

OTHER

179. Meece, Volney, ed. Telephone Service Directory. Edmond, OK: Foot-
      ball Writers Association of America. Annual. 197?-   .

This directory lists address and phone numbers of about 500 newspaper and magazine sportswriters covering football, with names geographically arranged. (Based on 1980 secondary source.)

13.
GOLF

BIBLIOGRAPHICAL SOURCES

180. Kennington, Donald. The Sourcebook of Golf. Phoenix, AZ: Oryx,
      1981. 255 p. illus. bibl. index. LC 81-11301.

      Comprehensive subject bibliographies on history, biography, fic-
      tion, business of golf, golf reference books, etc. Final chapter
      is a directory of golf associations in Britain and North America.
      Name, subject, and title indexes. (Based on 1982 secondary source.)

181. Murdoch, Joseph. Golf: A Guide to Information Sources. Sports,
      Games, and Pastimes Series, No. 7. Detroit, MI: Gale, 1979.
      232 p. index. LC 79-23270.

      This guide is divided into two main parts: part 1 deals only with
      books, while part 2 looks at such sources as golf periodicals, li-
      braries, golf courses, sources of instruction, etc. Indexes in-
      clude separate author, title, and subject.

182. Murdoch, Joseph S. The Library of Golf, 1743-1966. Detroit, MI:
      Gale, 1968. 314 p. illus. LC 67-29083.

      This bibliography begins with a history of golf literature, fol-
      lowed by the main body, which is a partially annotated list of
      books published on golf since 1743. Indexed by chronological per-
      iod, title, and subject.

BIOGRAPHICAL SOURCES

183. Elliott, Len, and Barbara Kelly. Who's Who in Golf. New Rochelle,
      NY: Arlington House, 1976. 208 p. LC 76-21059.

      An alphabetical register of past and present professional and ama-
      teur golfers who have won at least one tournament or have been se-
      lected for a major cup team. Each player receives about 10 - 20
      lines of biographical information.

184. Seitz, Nick. Superstars of Golf. New York: Simon & Schuster,
        1978. 192 p. illus. LC 77-92910.

An excellent source of in-depth biographical information on ten contemporary golfers selected both for money earned and charisma. The
photographs are unusually good.

DICTIONARIES

185. Adwick, Ken. Dictionary of Golf. New York: Drake, 1974. 201 p.
        illus. LC 74-10224.

The author's preface states that this book is designed as the
"golfing equivalent of the home doctor medical book - the one you
turn to when you are feeling below par." In an alphabetical arrangement, he addresses such topics as jitters, knees, maxims,
quack advice, tension, etc. A very specialized dictionary dealing
only with the individual and his/her golf game.

186. Davies, Peter. Davies' Dictionary of Golfing Terms. New York:
        Simon and Schuster, 1980. 188 p. illus. LC 80-13286.

Using the Oxford English Dictionary format, Davies defines the
term and then gives chronological listings of its use and origins.
Line drawings illustrate many of the definitions.

187. United States Golf Association. Dictionary of Golf Turfgrass
        Terms. Far Hills, NJ: Green Section, U.S. Golf Association,
        1980(?). 16 p.

A pamphlet-size dictionary of terms in usage among turf growers.

DIRECTORIES AND LOCATIONAL SOURCES

188. Directory of Amateur Golfers. 36 vols. (projected). Tucson, AZ:
        Amateur Golfers Association, 1976-   . illus. index. LC 76-
        377356.

A projected 36 volume set which lists the golf courses in each
state, includes location maps, color diagrams of the layout of each
course, plus fees, rules, ratings, local information, etc. (Examined: Arizona - Nevada - Utah volume.)

189. Miller, Dick. America's Greatest Golfing Resorts. Indianapolis,
        IN: Bobbs Merrill, 1977. 239 p. illus. bibl. LC 77-76822.

Arranged by categories (seaside, mountain, inland, desert), this
directory lists the author's personal choices for the 20 best golf
resorts in the country. Several pages of text and illustrations
try to capture the history and flavor of each course. Vital statistics are all packed in the back, and contain course and other
facilities information.

190. Ward-Thomas, Pat, et al. The World Atlas of Golf. New York:
      Random House, 1976. 280 p. illus. index. LC 76-10297.

      Divided into 6 world geographic regions, vivid color photographs
      and diagrams amplify the text for each course described. At the
      end the authors present a brief gazeteer of 100 additional out-
      standing golf courses with diagrams, statistics, and brief descrip-
      tions.

191. Van Daalen, Nicholas. The International Golf Guide: A Guide to
      the World's Most Exciting Golf Courses. Toronto, ONT: Pagurian
      Press, 1976. 190 p. illus. LC 77-361026.

      Arranged by country, this guide selects courses which have been
      deemed by experts and devotees as "most beautiful, most challenging,
      and toughest tests of golf." Although only a handful in each coun-
      try are annotated, others are listed and address given. Black and
      white photos highlight unusual features of specific courses.

ENCYCLOPEDIAS

192. Edmondson, Jolee. The Woman Golfer's Catalogue. New York: Stein
      and Day, 1980. 211 p. illus. index. LC 79-65116.

      Representative of a new genre in golf books - ones devoted to the
      problems peculiar to the women who play. Tips on grooming, cos-
      metics and nutrition are interspersed with brief biographies of
      famous women pros, a history of women's golf, colleges offering
      programs and scholarships, a glossary of terminology, a reading
      list, and amounts of money won in various tournaments. An excel-
      lent index increases the reference value of this very attractive
      book.

193. Evans, Webster. Encyclopaedia of Golf. New York: St. Martin's
      Press, 1974. 320 p. illus. index. LC 72-165470.

      Strong on British names and terms, this consists mainly of short-
      entry items in A - Z arrangement. It includes a section on rules
      and some pertinent statistical information on winners of particular
      tournaments or championships.

194. Ross, John M., ed. Golf Magazine's Encyclopedia of Golf. New
      York: Harper and Row, 1979. 439 p. illus. index. LC 77-11818.

      A collection of information about history, major tournament re-
      sults, biographies, golf equipment and principles, rules and eti-
      quette, some championship golf courses, and a glossary of golf
      terms.

195. Scott, Tom. The Concise Dictionary of Golf. New York: Mayflower
      Books, 1978. 256 p. LC 79-123718.

Divided into four main sections: players, courses, terms, and facts and figures. Lavishly illustrated, many full page color photos of specific players. Brief biographical sketches, while course information is lengthier and often includes diagrams of course layouts.

196.   Steel, Donald, and Peter Ryde. The Encyclopedia of Golf. New York: Viking, 1975. 480 p. illus. LC 73-17956.

An A - Z arrangement of terms, players, courses, tournaments, etc. all copiously illustrated. The last 50 pages are given over to tables telling who won what in the major competitions.

STATISTICAL SOURCES

197.   Dunhill World of Professional Golf. Ed. by Mark McCormack. San Diego, CA: A. S. Barnes. Annual. 1968-   .

There are several yearbooks of this type around, but this title was picked because it has become one of the standard statistical sources despite numerous title changes. It chronicles the results of all tournaments of any consequence in the world, and tries to assess the mood of the participants, the weather, and the unusual bits of drama present during specific tournaments. (Based on 1979 secondary source.)

198.   Golf Digest Annual. Norwalk, CT: Golf Digest. Annual. 1950-   . ISSN 0017-176X.

Each year's February issue contains this annual which recaps the previous year for both professionals and amateurs. In addition to a record book, such special features as golfers' unusual feats, places to play, new golf books, and a forecast for the upcoming season are regular features of the annual. (1970 through 1982 eds. examined.)

199.   Taylor, Dawson. The Masters: An Illustrated History. New York: A. S. Barnes, 1981. 223 p. illus. LC 72-6378.

Dedicated to documenting the Masters Tournament winners, the book begins with a history of the Augusta National Course, where it is played each year, then gives statistics and discussions of each tournament from 1934 through 1980. Photographs of each winner accompany the text, and additional statistics on the major tournament records of the Masters champions are included at the end of the book.

OTHER

200. Sheehan, Larry. The Whole Golf Catalog: Your Guide to All the
      Important Resources and Services in the World of Golf. New York:
      Atheneum, 1979. 292 p. illus. LC 78-20351

      This catalog is an amazing potpourri of information - from college
      golf scholarships to tournaments you can play in. There's a bit of
      instruction, equipment information, biography, bibliography and
      directory, all mixed together, making a good one-volume purchase.

14.
GYMNASTICS

201. Baer, Ursel. <u>Dictionary of Gymnastics Terminology in French - German - English</u>. Fort Worth, TX: United States Gymnastics Federation, 1978. 21 p.

French - German - English translations of gymnastics terms. (Based on 1982 secondary source.)

202. Hoyman, Annelis. <u>Modern Rhythmic Gymnastics Resources</u>. Fort Worth, TX: United States Gymnastics Federation, 1981. 8 p.

Partially annotated listing of books, records, and films on rhythmic gymnastics. Addresses of suppliers of books, records, and equipment also provided.

203. <u>NAGWS Guide - Gymnastics</u>. Reston, VA: The American Alliance for Health, Physical Education, Recreation and Dance. Biennial. 1963/65-   . illus. ISSN 0363-9282.

This source contains some information about the National Association for Girls and Women in Sport (NAGWS), as well as several articles on specific concerns in gymnastics, a 3 page bibliography of books, journals and A/V materials, and a section on officiating. The larger half of this source details with line drawings and descriptions the 1980-84 national compulsory routines for girls. (1982/84 ed. examined.)

204. Tatlow, Peter, ed. <u>The World of Gymnastics</u>. New York: Atheneum, 1978. 128 p. illus. bibl. index. LC 78-5389.

This source is a compilation of chapters/sections all written by gymnastics notables from various countries. Grouped into sections - "The Sport of Gymnastics," "Competitive Gymnastics," "The Movements," "Modern Rhythmic Gymnastics," and "Gymnastics Around the World" - are moderate length articles enhanced by many color and black and white photos. The section on women's and men's movements contains detailed explanations illustrated with line drawings. Over 10 countries are covered in the international section. One-page glossary and a subject index complete the work.

205. Who's Who in Gymnastics.   2nd ed.   Fort Worth, TX: United States
      Gymnastics Federation, 1977.

      Alphabetically arranged, this source contains over 350 biographical
      sketches of persons in gymnastics.   (Based on 1982 secondary
      source.)

15.
HOCKEY
(Includes Field and Ice Hockey)

Although ice hockey evolved from field hockey, the popularity of ice hockey is evidenced by the use of the term "hockey" to include ice hockey. This perhaps accounts for the lack of reference sources of U. S. or Canadian imprint for field hockey. The few titles selected are by no means of a true reference nature. They are, nevertheless, included if they provide such features as a glossary, records, directory, etc.

BIBLIOGRAPHICAL SOURCES

206. Saskatchewan Provincial Library. Bibliographic Services Division. Hockey: A Bibliography. Regina, SASK: Provincial Library, 1973. 21 p. index. LC 74-166310.

Lists over 100 one-line annotated titles of books from 1958 to 1973 on ice hockey available in the Provincial Library's collection. Arranged into 4 categories: history, technique, great teams, and biographies of famous stars. Author and title indexes.

207. Thom, Douglas J., and Tom Watt. The Hockey Bibliography: Ice Hockey Worldwide. OISE Bibliography Series #4. Toronto, ONT: Ontario Institute for Studies in Education and the Ministry of Culture and Recreation, 1978. 153 p. LC 78-324671.

About 2,500 entries are included of books, articles, audio-visual materials and research reports largely for the time period 1960-1978. European materials are included with translated titles. Arranged by type, i.e. statistical, periodical, etc. No indexes.

BIOGRAPHICAL SOURCES

208. The Complete Handbook of Pro Hockey. Ed. by Zander Hollander. New York: New American Library. Annual. 1971-   . illus.

Basically a biographical source on players grouped by the league they belong to. The last few chapters are devoted to statistics, with an official schedule for the year. (1981 ed. examined.)

209. Fischler, Stan, and Shirley Fischler. Fischlers' Ice Hockey Ency-
      clopedia. Rev. ed. New York: Crowell, 1979. 622 p. illus.
      LC 79-7640.

Biographical dictionary of over 700 players, owners and managers of American and Canadian teams. Brief descriptions on their career patterns and records. Also information on teams' history and major events. Portraits accompany entries for most athletes.

210. Hockey Stars Of... By Stan Fischer. New York: Pyramid Books.
      Irregular. 19?-   . illus. ISSN 0073-2869.

Biographical information which emphasizes players' performances in the latest season. The other sections reviewed the events of the past and latest seasons. The volume for each year is carried in the title, e.g., Hockey Stars of 1975. (1973 ed. examined.)

211. Hockey's Heritage. Toronto, ONT: Hockey Hall of Fame Governing
      Committee. Annual. 1969-   . illus. index. ISSN 0317-9257.

Brief biographies of Canadian Hall of Fame members in alphabetical order with portraits. (1978 ed. examined.)

212. Kariher, Harry C. Who's Who in Hockey. New Rochelle, NY: Arling-
      ton House, 1973. 189 p. LC 73-11868.

Complete biographical source book for pro and college hockey, with 600 entries on players, coaches, officials, etc. from 1870 to 1973.

213. Libby, Bill. Pro Hockey Heroes of Today. New York: Random House,
      1974. 150 p. illus. index. LC 74-4929.

Profiles of 24 top hockey stars in alphabetical order with more than 100 action photographs. Single author/subject index.

214. O'Brien, Andy. Superstars: Hockey's Greatest Players. Toronto,
      ONT: McGraw-Hill Ryerson Ltd., 1973. 188 p. illus. LC 73-
      10910.

Biographies of 19 players selected for an "all-time, superstar team." Arrangement is neither alphabetical nor chronological, but the table of contents with names of players serves as an index.

DICTIONARIES/ENCYCLOPEDIAS

215. Barnes, Mildred J. Field Hockey. The Coach and the Player. Bos-
      ton, MA: Allyn and Bacon, Inc., 1969. 262 p. illus. index.
      LC 69-17421.

Although not titled as an encyclopedia, this source is organized to serve as one for players and coaches. Terms are explained in considerable detail, and are grouped into chapters by play positions or moves, such as attack, defense, forward, goalkeeper, etc. Appendix provides a name list of outstanding U. S. players. Subject index.

216. Beddoes, Richard, Stan Fischler, and Ira Gitler. Hockey! The Story of the World's Fastest Sport. New exp. ed. New York: Macmillan, 1973. 387 p. illus. index. LC 72-176062.

This source provides information on the history, players, and games, with a chapter on the record breakers -- such as the longest game, biggest fight, worst goalie, etc. The appendix provides complete year-by-year team records and trophy winners. Single subject/name index.

217. Eskenazi, Gerald. Hockey. Chicago, IL: Follett, 1971. 224 p. illus. LC 70-166287.

Well illustrated introduction to the history of the sport through 1970-71 season, with information on the 14 teams in the National League. No index. (Based on 1972 secondary source.)

218. Gitler, Ira. Ice Hockey A to Z. New York: Lothrop, Lee and Shepard, 1978. 157 p. illus. LC 78-8482.

A combination of dictionary and handbook on ice hockey, non-hockey specific terms, such as luck, Indians, movies, X-rays and injuries are included to bring forth discussions of the game, its history and players. Poorly executed photos.

219. Hollander, Zander, and Hal Bock, eds. The Complete Encyclopedia of Ice Hockey. Rev. ed. Englewood Cliffs, NJ: Prentice Hall, 1974. 702 p. illus. index. LC 73-15019.

An established reference work in its field, this includes information on the World Hockey Association, records, rules, Hall of Fame, etc. Black and white photos only. Similar in the extent and quality of coverage to Ronberg's Hockey Encyclopedia (#221). (Based on 1976 secondary source.)

220. Lees, Josephine T., and Betty Shellenberger. Field Hockey. 2nd ed. New York: Ronald Press Co., 1969. 147 p. illus. index. LC 69-14673.

Similar in organization to Mildred J. Barnes' Field Hockey (#215), with lots of photos to clarify the descriptions. A most useful feature is the glossary of field hockey terms. Subject index.

221. Ronberg, Gary. The Hockey Encyclopedia. New York: Macmillan, 1974. 392 p. illus. LC 73-21297.

This contains biographies, rosters, history, record book -- all in
one volume. The general history chapter is supplemented by biographies on important coaches and executives. It documents the
most significant games, the team dynasties, Hall of Fame members,
etc. Arrangement is topical, with the table of contents providing
the only means of page references. Color photos.

222. Spencer, David and Barbara Spencer. The Pocket Hockey Encyclopedia.
     Rev. & updated ed. New York: Charles Scribner's, 1976. 210 p.
     LC 77-352786.

A source book for statistics, jargon, rules and information on
players. Hockey terms are cross-indexed with the Official National
Hockey League rules. Also included is history of leagues and cups.

223. Styer, Robert A. The Encyclopedia of Hockey. New and rev. ed.
     South Brunswick, NJ: A. S. Barnes, 1973. 412 p. illus. LC
     72-5182.

Contents are grouped into 21 chapters, from evolution of hockey
to 1972-73 season, with the table of contents serving as an index.
Included are the league records, cup records, registry of players
and goaltenders, champions, and rule changes up to 1972. A special feature is diagrams of major hockey team stadiums.

STATISTICAL SOURCES

224. Hockey Register. St. Louis, MO: Sporting News. Annual.
     1972-   . illus. ISSN 0090-2292.

Organized into three broad sections -- forwards and defensemen,
goaltenders, and retired players -- yearly statistics are provided
for each player up through the prior season. Arrangement within
sections is alphabetical by player's name. Photos provided only
for players who retired in prior season. Complements Pro and Amateur Hockey Guide (#231), which, among other things, provides records for teams and leagues. (1981-82 ed. examined.)

225. Petersen's Pro Hockey. Los Angeles, CA: Petersen Publishing Co.
     Annual. 1980-   . illus. index. ISSN 0271-2636.

This annual publication includes information on performance, rule
changes, past season statistics, etc. (Based on 1980 secondary
source.)

226. Spencer, David. The New Professional Hockey Almanac. Toronto, ONT:
     Pagurian Press, 1978. 192 p. illus.

A record book of histories of NHL and Stanley Cup statistics and
rules. Statistical data are organized into over 100 categories,
such as fastest, highest, most, fewest, etc. for the league and for
individuals.

OTHER

227. NAGWS Guide: Field Hockey - Lacrosse. Washington, DC: National
Alliance for Girls and Women in Sport, American Alliance for
Health, Physical Education and Recreation. Biennial.
1950-52-   . illus. bibl. ISSN 0145-9554.

Field hockey and Lacrosse each has its own section, most of which
contains rules and signed articles on history, technique, and tips.
Of reference value are the directory of national and international
association officials, bibliographies, list of visual aids, equipment specifications, and members of U. S. teams in the World Championship Games. (Formerly Official Field Hockey - Lacrosse Guide,
1950-76.) (1976-78 ed. examined.)

228. NCAA Ice Hockey. Shawnee Mission, KS: National Collegiate Athletic Association. Annual. 1926-   . illus. index. ISSN
0734-5011.

First half of this guide begins with a national preview-review of
college teams by division, followed by the up-coming season's schedule, and then records of the preceding year. The second half is
the official rules section with rules on teams and penalties. Includes Code of Ethics for coaches and a list of collegiate hockey's
Hall of Fame members. Index to rules. (Formerly Official National
Collegiate Athletic Association Ice Hockey Guide, 1944-1979.)
(1982 ed. examined.)

229. National Hockey League Guide. Montreal, QUE: National Hockey
League. Annual. 1965-   . index. ISSN 0316-8174.

Organized into seven sections, this directory and statistical source
covers the team rosters, champions, schedules, etc. of National
Hockey League, American Hockey League, and Central Professional
Hockey League, as well as biographies of players. It absorbs the
NHL Press and Radio Guide and the NHL Stanley Cup Records and Sta-
tistics. (1979 ed. examined.)

230. Official Guide of the Amateur Hockey Association of the United
States. Colorado Springs, CO: Amateur Hockey Association of the
United States. Annual. 19?-   . illus. ISSN 0516-8635.

This guide provides information on names and addresses of officials,
all-time and past season winners for all divisions, discussions of
the Canada Cup, World Championship, etc. (Based on 1977 secondary
source.)

231. Pro and Amateur Hockey Guide. St. Louis, MO: The Sporting News.
Annual. 1968-   . illus. ISSN 0079-550X.

Directory and record book of American and Canadian hockey leagues
and World Hockey Association, including junior and college leagues.
Information on each team's home ice rink, address, complete individual scoring and goaltending record, and attendance figures for
some games. Also names of draftees for the expansion and entry
drafts. Continues Pro and Senior Hockey Guide. (1979-80 ed. examined.)

232. Pro Hockey. Ed. by Jim Proudfoot. New York: Simon and Schuster.
      Annual. 1968-   . illus. ISSN 0079-5569.

Analysis of each team in the National Hockey League, its past season's performance, and strengths and weaknesses of individual players. Includes names of NHL officers, address, and team color.
Separate chapters dealing with individuals' scores by teams and
Hall of Fame. (1977-78 ed. examined.)

16.
LaCROSSE

233. Canadian Lacrosse Association Coaching Committee. Lacrosse Catalogue. Vanier, ONT: Canadian Lacrosse Association, 1981. (20
u.p.) (SIRC GV 489 #12203).

Over 60 titles and prices of books, films, videotapes, cassettes
on lacrosse are listed.

234. Fusting, Eugene M., ed. Star-Sticks. Baltimore, MD: Summer House
Publications, 1979. 242 p. illus. LC 79-64888.

A compilation of articles by famous lacrosse players on their career, philosophy, and technique of plays. Each article is accompanied by a photo and the editor's biographical sketch of the star.
Players are grouped by their play positions. Not a traditional reference book.

235. NAGWS Guide: Field Hockey - Lacrosse. Washington, DC: National
Association for Girls & Women in Sport, American Alliance of
Health, Physical Education, and Recreation. Biennial. 1958/60-
. illus. bibl. ISSN 0145-9554.

(See annotation for item #227.)

236. NCAA Lacrosse. Shawnee Mission, KS: National Collegiate Athletic
Association. Annual. 19?- . illus. ISSN 0732-9059.

This guide provides a preview-review of college team records of the
preceding year and a schedule. The rule section includes rule
changes. (Formerly Official National Collegiate Athletic Association Lacrosse Guide, 19?-1979.) (1980 ed. examined.)

17.
MARTIAL ARTS

BIOGRAPHICAL SOURCES

237. Smith, Robert W. Chinese Boxing: Masters and Methods. New York:
      Kodansha International, 1974. 141 p. illus. bibl. LC 73-79767.

      Narrative descriptions of about 20 Chinese boxers and their methods
      that the author observed in the 1960's. Several appendixes, includ-
      ing one listing the kinds of Chinese boxing and titles of films de-
      picting the types, and a Chinese - English glossary of terms.

238. Wall, Bob. Who's Who in the Martial Arts and Directory of Black
      Belts. Beverly Hills, CA: R. A. Wall Investments, Inc., 1975.
      254 p. illus. LC 75-22880.

      About 130 one-page biographies of contemporary U. S. men and women
      who have made contributions to the positive growth of the martial
      arts in 3 of several areas (instruction, business, promotion, com-
      petition, etc.). Directory of black belts, arranged by state and
      then city, primarily provides names and addresses of those connected
      with martial arts schools and academies. Brief dictionary of terms
      in front.

DICTIONARIES/ENCYCLOPEDIAS

239. Farkas, Emil, and John Corcoran. The Overlook Martial Arts Dic-
      tionary. Woodstock, NY: Overlook Press, 1981. 288 p. bibl.
      LC 81-47415.

      Quite comprehensive in scope and clearly worded definitions.
      (Based on 1981 secondary source.)

240. Shapiro, Amy. Running Press Glossary of Martial Arts Languages.
      Philadelphia, PA: Running Press, 1978. 112 p. LC 77-12635.

Choice of terminology and definitions provided reveal a much
briefer, less authoritative coverage of the subject than that found
in #241, The Martial Arts Encyclopedia.

241. Winderbaum, Larry. The Martial Arts Encyclopedia. Washington, DC:
        Inscape Pub., 1977. 215 p. illus. bibl. LC 76-43250.

In an A - Z arrangement, entries cover almost all aspects of the
fighting arts, biographical information about the great teachers
and practitioners, etc. Many black and white drawings, photographs,
maps, and charts. Includes excellent one-page chronology of the development of the martial arts. Three appendixes discuss the topics
"Selecting a Commercial School," "The Martial Arts in the Colleges,"
and "Women in the Martial Arts." Brief, unannotated bibliography.

OTHER

242. Domblant, Raymond, et al. Results Digest Judo. Ottawa, ONT: Judo
        Canada, 1980. unpaged.

Historical record of the names and nationalities of winners for the
following judo competitions: Olympic Games, World Championships,
All Japan Championships, Pan American Games and Championships,
European Championships, International Competitions, Canada Cup and
Games, and Canadian Championships. Arranged by competition. Re-
sults provided for annual ones through 1980.

243. Logan, William, and Herman Petras. Handbook of the Martial Arts
        and Self-Defense. New York: Funk & Wagnalls, 1975. 282 p.
        illus. bibl. LC 74-26776.

Separate chapters on aikido, judo, karate, and kung fu provide history, description, and technique. Also chapters on self-defense
for women. Many photos. Appendixes include belt rankings, further readings, and national directory of schools and equipment.

18.
RUGBY

244. Jones, John R., comp. <u>Encyclopedia of Rugby Union Football.</u> 3rd
ed. Rev. and ed. by Maurice Golesworthy. London, ENG: Robert
Hale, 1976. 185 p. illus. index. LC 77-353873.

Organized in an A to Z format, terms, individual and team records,
and biographies are treated in entries of varying lengths. Over
10 pages are devoted to tours in chronological order from 1888 to
1975, giving the score, players' names by playing positions, and
manager's name. History, laws of the game, and such trivia as
oldest player, famous incidents involving referees, etc. are included. Portraits and action photos only of British and New Zealand players.

245. Powell, John T. <u>Inside Rugby - The Team Game.</u> Chicago, IL: Henry
Regnery Co., 1976. 102 p. illus. index. LC 76-6281.

In thirteen 2 - 3 page chapters this source explains and illustrates
with action photos the various terms related to types of maneuvers
(passing and receiving, running, etc.) or positions (forwards,
backs, etc.). Beginning with a short history of the games, other
chapters focus on descriptions of the field, equipment, and laws
the game. A glossary defines terms that are non-specific. Subject
index.

246. Prusmack, A. Jon. <u>Rugby: A Guide for Players, Coaches, and Spectators.</u> New York: Hawthorn Books Inc., 1979. 182 p. illus. index. LC 78-65604.

Organized into 7 chapters are fundamentals of particular playing positions and techniques. Under each, terms are briefly described and
illustrated with plates and diagrams. It also includes history and
rules of the game.

19.
RUNNING

These sources provide reference information for running as a sport, distinct from the various track and field running events, although one title (#251) provides information for both of these aspects of running. Sources for track and field running events are located in the section "Track and Field."

DIRECTORIES AND LOCATIONAL SOURCES

247. D'Alton, Martina. The Runner's Guide to the U. S. A.. New York: Summit Books, 1978. 410 p. illus. LC 78-10315.

Arranged by geographical section, this source provides background and vital information on established U. S. races. A general description, entry requirements, starting point, course details, weather, altitude, awards, sponsors, and name of running club and race contacts to write for further information comprise each entry. About half of the race descriptions are accompanied with maps of the course. Appendices have listings of running associations, periodicals and a race calendar.

248. Roth, Peter. Running USA: The Complete Guide to Running in 125 American Cities. New York: Aardvark, 1979. 333 p. illus. LC 79-750.

Listed first by state, then alphabetically by city, descriptive overview, climatological data, hotels located near running courses, and course descriptions are provided. Also listed are available outdoor and indoor tracks, running clubs, names and dates of races, and names, addresses and phone numbers of contacts. Many courses have maps adjoining descriptions.

249. Tewsley, Bob. Where to Run In Canada. Ottawa, ONT: Deneau and Greenberg Pub., 1980. 181 p. illus.

For 23 Canadian cities, this source provides maps locating running routes, brief description of the city (weather, transportation, hotels), and detailed descriptions of the routes.

STATISTICAL SOURCES

250. Runner's Almanac. Mountain View, CA: World Publications. Annual.
       1972-   . illus.

      Divided into four major sections which provide: 1) review of pre-
      vious season's record breakers and major race winners, 2) listing
      of athletic associations that sponsor running events and all col-
      lege conferences, 3) running records in all divisions, and 4) an
      extensive directory, arranged by state (including Canada), of places
      to race with names and addresses of race contacts, background in-
      formation on the locale, etc. (Based on 1979 secondary source.)

251. Runner's World Annual. Mountain View, CA: Runner's World Magazine
       Co. Annual. 1981-   . illus. ISSN 0035-9939.

      The annual is the 13th issue of the monthly magazine Runner's
      World. The 1981 annual contains 20 pages of records for the top
      marathon times of 1980 for men and women registered in U. S. and
      Canadian marathons. Also included are world records for track and
      field events, both all-time records and for 1980. Much descriptive
      information is provided about races in North America. (1981 ed.
      examined.)

20.
SHOOTING

CATALOGS

252. Gun Digest. Northfield, IL: Digest Books. Annual. 1944- .
      illus. index. ISSN 0072-9034.

      Although the catalog section, which is devoted to reviewing new
      products, is quite large, this source also contains articles, an-
      notated list of books, a periodical listing, arms associations in
      the U. S. and abroad, and a list of manufacturers. The illustrated
      new products section is arranged by type of gun, with a section on
      sights and scopes. (Based on 1979 secondary source.)

253. Redbook of Used Gun Values: Including the Gun Buyer's Directory.
      Skokie, IL: Guns Magazine. Annual. 1955- . ISSN 0484-1687.

254. Shooter's Bible. So. Hackensack, NJ: Stoeger Pub. Co. Annual.
      1925?- . illus. index.

      The 1982 edition (No. 73) includes the major section, a complete,
      illustrated catalog of firearms and accessories currently available
      on the American market; a reference section with directory informa-
      tion for weapons and military museums of North America; list of or-
      ganizations and associations; a bibliography of books and magazines;
      a directory of manufacturers and suppliers; and a section contain-
      ing 5 - 10 page articles on a variety of topics. A highly regarded
      and comprehensive reference work. (1982 ed. examined.)

DICTIONARIES/ENCYCLOPEDIAS

255. Mueller, Chester, and John Olson. Shooter's Bible Small Arms Lexi-
      con and Concise Encyclopedia. So. Hackensack, NJ: Shooter's
      Bible, 1968. 309 p. LC 67-30798.

Over 3,000 phrases, words, and names that comprise the firearms
language are defined. Also included are biographical briefs of
well known persons in the development of firearms. An appendix contains 25 tables and charts of useful data for equivalents measures,
dates in firearms history, etc. A 29 page supplement of later entries completes the dictionary.

256. Nonte, George C., Jr. Firearms Encyclopedia. New York: Harper
      and Row, 1973. 341 p. illus. index. LC 73-80712.

An authoritative and comprehensive A through Z coverage of all terms
relating to firearms and their use and development. Precise details on aspects of competition and the rifles used. An annotated
bibliography of books and a lengthy appendix containing many useful
directories (e.g., arms associations, suppliers, etc.) enhance this
source's reference value.

257. Sparano, Vin T. Complete Outdoors Encyclopedia. 2nd ed. New York:
      Harper and Row, 1980. 607 p. illus. index. LC 72-90934.

Although most of the material in this source is outside our scope,
this is included because Part I (about 145 pages) is composed of articles on firearms and shooting -- e.g., competition shooting, skeet
shooting, and selection of handguns. Precise explanations and information are complemented by extensive use of illustrations that
depict shooting positions, etc.

OTHER

258. National Rifle Association Collegiate Shooting Sports Directory.
      2nd ed. Washington, DC: National Rifle Association, 1981.
      100 p. bibl.

Geographically arranged, this source lists and describes about 155
shooting programs in U. S. colleges and universities. Several articles on aspects of collegiate shooting programs have been added
to this second edition.

21.
SKATING, ICE

259. Heller, Mark, ed. <u>The Illustrated Encyclopedia of Ice Skating</u>.
New York: Paddington Press, 1979. 223 p. illus. index. bibl.
LC 79-14633.

Comprehensive guide to the rules, background and practice of every
skating discipline and sport -- figure skating, pair skating, ice
dancing, touring and speed skating. Also includes full explanation
of every ice rink sport: curling, Eisschiessen, bandy, and ice
hockey. Reference section has a three-language glossary of skating
terms, and a complete list of World and Olympic champions.

260. Stephenson, Lois, and Richard Stephenson. <u>A History and Annotated
Bibliography of Skating Costume</u>. Meriden, CT: Bayberry Hill
Press, 1970. 101 p. illus. bibl. LC 70-26277.

22.
SKIING

BIBLIOGRAPHICAL SOURCES

261. Bunja, Patricia A. <u>Informational Resources on Downhill Skiing</u>.
    Pittsburgh, PA: unpublished, 1979. 39 p. index. (SIRC GV 854
    #9763).

    This alphabetical-by-name bibliography resulted as part of the au-
    thor's M.A. thesis requirements. Includes journal articles, books,
    and films, primarily from the mid-1960's through 1978 which focus
    on alpine skiing technique, competition, equipment, injuries, and
    training methods. International coverage. Broad subject index.

262. Forkes, David. <u>Skiing: An English Language Bibliography 1891-1971</u>.
    Vancouver, BC: unpublished, 1975. 53 p. index. (SIRC GV 854
    #8885).

    Arranged chronologically with author and title indexes, this bib-
    liography includes only English language books. Locations are pro-
    vided for many of the older titles.

263. Goeldner, Charles R. and Karen P. Dicke. <u>Bibliography of Skiing
    Studies</u>. 6th ed. Boulder, CO: Business Research Division Gradu-
    ate School of Business Administration, University of Colorado,
    1982. 96 p.

    This specialized bibliography has improved greatly from earlier edi-
    tions. The type is better and the annotations contain full biblio-
    graphic information for ordering or loan. Its stated purpose is to
    describe studies that are available on the skiing industry, charac-
    teristics of skiers, skiing's economic impact, financial opera-
    tions, and future. It is divided into 3 sections: public studies
    (e.g. "Characteristics of Central New York Skiiers"), private stu-
    dies (e.g. "Colorado Ski Areas' Wage and Salary Survey: 1979-80
    Ski Season") and theses/dissertations (e.g. "Location Analysis of
    High-Volume Skiing in Western U. S."). Largest share of citations
    cover Colorado, but other areas are represented as well.

DIRECTORIES AND LOCATIONAL SOURCES

264.   Fehr, Lucy. Cross Country Skiing: A Guide to America's Best Trails.
        Americans-Discover-America Series. New York: Morrow, 1979.
        198 p. illus. LC 79-90099.

        Arrangement is alphabetical by state, and alphabetical within the
        state. Each entry gives basic trail information plus address and
        phone numbers to write for specific details. Fehr also has another
        book in this series, Skiing USA, which is the downhill companion to
        this volume.

265.   Keating, Michael. Michael Keating's Cross Country Canada: Hand-
        book and Trail Guide for Cross Country Skiers. New York: Van
        Nostrand Reinhold, 1977. 212 p. illus. LC 76-29501.

        An introductory section deals with such topics as equipment, winter
        survival, and the elements of winter. The bulk of the book is a di-
        rectory of trails arranged by province. Each contains some pre-
        liminary information, such as mean temperatures and location maps,
        then describes the individual trail areas.

266.   The White Book of Ski Areas: U. S. and Canada. Washington, DC:
        Inter-Ski Services Inc. Annual. 1978-   . ISSN 0163-9684.

        For each state or province, a map is provided which contains ski
        locations keyed into descriptive information. Information given in-
        cludes: skiing statistics, costs/instruction, lodging/services/
        travel information, and special area comments, e.g. Greek Peak in
        N.Y. has an excellent program for handicapped persons. (1978 ed.
        examined.)

ENCYCLOPEDIAS

267.   Berry, I. William. The Great North American Ski Book. Rev. and up-
        dated ed. New York: Scribner's, 1982. bibl. illus. LC 82-
        6029.

        The editors of Ski Magazine have produced this comprehensive book
        on the history, equipment, techniques, and competitive aspects of
        the sport. Appendices contain a directory of ski slopes, a glossary
        of terms, a list of ski organizations, a chronology of ski develop-
        ments, and a bibliography of books, journals, and films. (1973 ed.
        examined.)

268.   Heller, Mark. The Skier's Encyclopedia. New York: Paddington
        Press, 1979. 287 p. illus. bibl. index. LC 79-9151.

        Much of this book falls in the general category of information on
        equipment, techniques, etc. Last 40 pages contain reference ma-
        terial: glossary, Olympic statistics, selected bibliography, and
        an index.

269. Miller, Peter. Peter Miller's Ski Almanac. New York: Doubleday,
      1979. 307 p. illus. LC 79-7660.

A comprehensive approach to lessons, equipment, resorts, clothing,
snow and avalanche information, etc. It includes a directory of
professional and amateur associations and manufacturers, as well as
a bibliography of books, periodicals, and movies. Two sections
especially worth noting are the still and film photography chapter,
and the one which compares and evaluates the major serial ski publications. About the only thing this title lacks is an index to
tie it all together.

270. Needham, Richard, ed. Ski Magazine's Encyclopedia of Skiing. Rev.
      and updated. New York: Harper and Row, 1979. 452 p. illus.
      index. LC 77-11803.

Organized into six main sections, this standard source begins with
a history of skiing which includes a chronological "highlights of
skiing" from 1849-1978, then sections II - IV concentrate on equipment, principles of skiing, and major competitions, respectively.
The last two sections combine a directory of ski resorts and tra-
veling tips with a glossary of skiing terms, a list of the ski associations of the world, and a multilingual lexicon of useful skiing terms.

STATISTICAL SOURCES

271. The Canadian Ski Council. Canadian Ski Industry. n.p. 1979?.
      115 p. (SIRC GV 854.8 .C3 #10681).

A statistical report that synthesizes data from 9 surveys about
the Canadian skier (number of, frequency of participation, etc.);
ski areas (facilities, season performance, costs); ski instruction
(programs offered, instructors, revenue); ski equipment market (im-
ports, sales, rentals); and the American skiing tourist.

272. Goeldner, C. R. and Ted Farwell. Economic Analysis of North Ameri-
      can Ski Areas. Boulder, CO: Business Research Division, Gradu-
      ate School of Business Administration, University of Colorado.
      Irregular. 1974?-   .

The best statistics on the U. S. ski industry's economic impact and
importance have been coming out of the University of Colorado's
Business Research Center. This title has appeared every year or
two since about 1974, and it represents one of many such studies
available through the University of Colorado. (Based on 1981 secondary source.)

273. Ski Racing Redbook. Fair Haven, VT: Ski Racing Inc. Annual.
      19? -   . illus. ISSN 0091-1461.

This source summarizes the information found in the periodical Ski
Racing for each season. It presents a statistical summary of the
winners of the major competitions, then profiles the major newsma-
kers for that particular season. (1981-82 ed. examined.)

23.
SOCCER

BIOGRAPHICAL SOURCES

274. Hill, Jimmy. Great Soccer Stars. New York: Hamlyn, 1978. 176 p. illus. LC 79-310999.

One- to two-page career biographies of 100 great soccer stars, with action photographs of each player.

275. Tyler, Martin. Soccer: The World Game. New York: St. Martin's Press, 1978. 185 p. illus. index. LC 78-2982.

This source serves as both a history of the game and its various world cup competitions, and an anecdotal account of 19 soccer super-stars. Index makes the information easy to access.

DICTIONARIES

276. Considine, Tim. The Photographic Dictionary of Soccer. New York: Warner Books, 1979. 208 p. illus. LC 79-109041.

Black and white photographs illustrate the most important terms and concepts in soccer. In addition, the author has included the laws of the game and various decisions of the International Board. (Based on 1980 secondary source.)

277. Sirges, Horst. Elsevier's Football Dictionary: English/German, German/English. Amsterdam; New York: Elsevier Scientific, 1980. 286 p. LC 80-14335.

Lists part of speech, gives very brief definitions, then equivalent in the other language.

ENCYCLOPEDIAS

278. Henshaw, Richard. The Encyclopedia of World Soccer. Washington, DC: New Republic Books, 1979. 828 p. illus. bibl. LC 78-26570.

   Entries appear in alphabetical order and vary in length from a one-line definition on "infringements" to 37 pages of text and statistics on the World Championship - FIFA World Cup. Biographies of famous soccer players are interspersed with facts, definitions, and histories of soccer in various countries.

279. Hollander, Zander. The American Encyclopedia of Soccer. New York: Everest House, 1980. 544 p. illus. index. LC 79-51205.

   In three major sections this source opens with a history of soccer and its introduction to North America. The next section surveys the college game from 1900-1978 in narrative form, followed by college records. The final section covers the professionals, describing the American Soccer League, the North American Soccer League, and the World Cup. In this section are two useful chapters in which are listed the NASL records and the all-time NASL player register through 1979. Includes glossary and laws of the game.

280. Rote, Kyle, Jr. Kyle Rote Jr.'s Complete Book of Soccer. New York: Simon and Schuster, 1978. 300 p. illus. bibl. index. LC 77-16625.

   The growing popularity of soccer in North America has contributed to books like this one which seek to define and explain its world following. Rote sprinkles statistics throughout the first half of the book, then devotes 7 appendices to statistics, a glossary of terms, laws, and signals.

STATISTICAL SOURCES

281. The Complete Handbook of Soccer. Ed. by Zander Hollander. Bergenfield, NJ: New American Library. Annual. 1976-   . illus. ISSN 0363-6046.

   Provides assessments of teams' seasons based on personnel, past records, etc. Hollander covers professional, collegiate, and high school soccer, then includes the statistics from the previous season. Photographs and statistics on various players make this a useful source. (1980 ed. examined.)

282. Golesworthy, Maurice. The Encyclopedia of Association Football. 12th ed. London, ENG: Robert Hale, 1976. 239 p. illus. index.

Much more a statistical source than an encyclopedia, this British title represents a source which has become a standard in the field. Golesworthy uses an A - Z format and packs the book full of statistics on such topics as individual goal scoring, international match results, and even the effect of the weather on specific past seasons. Brief career profiles of selected players are also included.

283. The Official North American Soccer League Guide. St. Louis, MO: Sporting News. Annual? 1968-   . illus. ISSN 0549-7094.

Team records are listed for the prior season along with a schedule for the next season. Also includes a variety of NASL records and attendance figures, all-time scoring leaders and stars, and historical records for individual players. NASL history, staff, officials and condensed rules also provided. (1981 ed. examined.)

284. NCAA Soccer. Shawnee Mission, KS: National Collegiate Athletic Association. Annual. 1927/28-   . ISSN 0195-7457.

Results of the previous season, schedules for the current one, names of NCAA officials nationwide, and an official rules section comprise the contents of this annual guide. (Formerly the Official National Collegiate Athletic Association Soccer Guide, 1927-1979.) (1980 ed. examined.)

285. Rollin, Jack. The Guinness Book of Soccer Facts and Feats. 2nd ed. Enfield, ENG: Guinness Superlatives Ltd., 1979. 251 p. illus. index. LC 80-465139.

Most of this book chronicles the happenings in British, European, and world soccer. It is packed with such statistics as British pre-war League goalscorers, major records and attendance figures, and growth of the world governing body FIFA.

24.
SWIMMING

BIBLIOGRAPHICAL SOURCES

286. Chiasson, Gilles, comp. <u>Ten Years of English Books on Swimming</u>. Ottawa, ONT: Sport Information Resource Center, 1976. 26 p. (SIRC GV 837 #7298).

English language books and theses published between 1965-75 are listed by title. Has author index, but no subject access.

287. Council for National Cooperation in Aquatics. <u>Swimming and Diving: A Bibliography</u>. New York: Association Press, 1968. 264 p. LC 68-31332.

A computer-generated bibliography arranged by 14 broad subject categories and sub-divided by type of material (e.g., competitive swimming - films). This bibliography begins where a previous one left off in 1938 and extends coverage through 1966. Hopefully, a newer edition will be forthcoming. It represents a standard source compiled by a major association in the field of swimming.

STATISTICAL SOURCES

288. <u>American Swimmer: The Official Book of Swimming Records</u>. Los Angeles, CA: Swimming World, 1976. 216 p. LC 76-45702.

Records from world, Olympic, American, European, NCAA, AAU, NAIA, YMCA, AIAW, junior college, and high school competitions. Produced by the editors of <u>Swimming World</u> magazine.

289. <u>NAGWS Guide - Competitive Swimming and Diving</u>. Reston, VA: American Alliance for Health, Physical Education, Recreation, and Dance. National Association for Girls and Women in Sport. Annual. 1949-   .

NAGWS information on standards and composition of rule committee, official rules, and officiating policies. Separate section for AIAW championship results and policies, and one for NAGWS records. (1980/81 ed. examined.)

290. NAGWS Guide - Synchronized Swimming. Reston, VA: American Alliance for Health, Physical Education, Recreation, and Dance. National Association for Girls and Women in Sport. Annual. 1949/51-   . illus. ISSN 0163-4267.

Information about NAGWS, its standards and committee composition, official rules, procedures for officiating, and collegiate championship results (with photos) for the previous year. (1980/81 ed. examined.)

291. NCAA Swimming. Shawnee Mission, KS: National Collegiate Athletic Association. Annual. 1915/16-   . ISSN 0272-8095.

First half of the book covers men's and women's championship and other meet results. Last half contains official rules. (Previously titled Official National Collegiate Athletic Association Swimming Guide, 1915/16-1979.) (Based on 1979 secondary source.)

292. Swimming and Diving Rules and Records. Elgin, IL: National Federation of State High School Associations. Annual. 19?-   .

This source has been expanded to include records: state meet results for previous season; all-time winners for boy's high school, girl's high school, prep school; and National Interscholastic Swimming. (Continues Swimming Rules.) (Based on 1979 secondary source.)

OTHER

293. Besford, Pat, comp. Encyclopaedia of Swimming. 2nd ed. New York: St. Martin's Press, 1976. 302 p. illus. index. LC 76-16687.

Arranged in standard dictionary format, with all aspects and organizations of competitive swimming and diving covered. Greater emphasis is given to the British Commonwealth, however. Includes records and biographical sketches.

25.
TENNIS
(Includes Racquetball and Squash)

BIBLIOGRAPHICAL SOURCES

294. Peele, David A. Racket and Paddle Games: A Guide to Information
Sources. Sports, Games, and Pastimes Information Guide Series,
No. 9. Detroit, MI: Gale, 1980. 241 p. index. LC 80-23977.

Annotated bibliography of books, films, organizations, and periodicals about tennis, racquetball, table tennis, squash, platform tennis, paddleball, and badminton. Of special interest is the final
short chapter, "Recommended Purchases for Libraries and Individuals." Four indexes -- author, title, subject and association.

295. Racquet and Tennis Club, New York Library. A Dictionary Catalogue
of the Library of Sports in the Racquet and Tennis Club, with
Special Collections on Tennis, Lawn Tennis and Early American
Sport. 2 vols. Boston, MA: G. K. Hall, 1970. LC 78-166482.

A dictionary-style author and subject catalog of over 14,300 books
and pamphlets in the Club's library. Includes titles on all sports
and games from ancient time to the 20th century. The collection is
particularly strong in tennis, lawn tennis, and early American
sports. A list of subject headings preceding the main catalog provides cross references to appropriate tennis entries.

296. United States Tennis Association Film List. Princeton, NJ: USTA
Education and Research Center. Annual. 1971- .

Organized by formats (e.g., 16 mm, super 8 mm, 35 mm filmstrips,
and videotapes), and sub-categorized as instructional, match highlights, or tennis miscellany, this source identifies, describes,
and lists sources for rental and/or purchase for over 100 films.
USTA film libraries, 16 mm free-loan film services, and film distributors are also listed. (1979 ed. examined.)

CATALOGS

297. Duggan, Moira, and Eugene Scott. The Tennis Catalog. New York:
Macmillan, 1978. 256 p. illus. bibl. LC 77-17869.

A guide to the tennis marketplace with 16 chapters, each covering
one major item. For most equipment listed, there is a photograph,
description, and price. Also has sections on possible careers in
tennis, resorts and camps, a selection of books, films, and periodicals, and a list of mail order houses.

298. Fiott, Steve. Tennis Equipment. Rev. and enlarged ed. Radnor,
PA: Chilton, 1978. 224 p. illus. LC 77-014726.

Weak and strong points are detailed in text, supplemented with photos, about the manufacture and "playability" of different brands of
rackets, shoes, balls, strings, and a brief section on clothing.

299. Tennis Directory. Boston, MA: Ski Earth Publications. Semiannual.
1977-   . illus.

Manufacturers of tennis equipment, court lighting equipment, tennis apparel, ball machines, and stringing machines are classified
by product. Entries provide name and address of companies and product descriptions. Also includes some feature articles and a detailed listing of camps and resorts. (Based on 1980 secondary
source.)

DIRECTORIES AND LOCATIONAL SOURCES

300. McShirley, Susan. Racquetball: Where to Play U. S. A. 2nd ed.
Los Angeles, CA: S. R. M. Press, 1979. 344 p. LC 79-56757.

Arranged alphabetically by state, this directory uses symbols to
indicate additional services (e.g., child care), and gives addresses, hours, locations, and guest policy.

301. Official United States Tennis Tournament Directory. Ann Arbor, MI:
U. S. Tennis Survey, Inc. Annual. 1977-   . ISSN 0145-7977.

Section A is a list of individual tournaments organized by state and
by date of start of play. Section B is an alphabetical list of cir-
cuits, USTA National championships and the World Team Tennis schedule for the current year. Section C provides names and addresses
of major U. S. tennis organizations. Section D lists names and addresses of about 25 tennis magazines and newspapers. (1978/79 ed.
examined.)

302. United States Professional Tennis Association Directory. Sarasota,
FL: U. S. Professional Tennis Association. Annual. 19?-   .
index.

This source provides names and addresses for about 3,000 professional and amateur tennis players, coaches, and others active in the
sport. Also includes a calendar of events, USPTA by-laws, and USPTA
rankings and sanctioned tournaments. Division index. (Based on
1980 secondary source.)

303. United States Tennis Association's College Tennis Guide. Princeton, NJ: U. S. Tennis Association. Biennial. 1978-   .

Arranged alphabetically by state, information about nearly 1,500
U. S. college and junior college tennis, inter-collegiate tennis
teams and scholarships is provided. Also listed are numbers of
courts, names of coaches, and rankings. (1978 ed. examined.)

304. Van Daalen, **Nicholas**. The New International Tennis Guide: A Guide
to Some of the Most Exciting Tennis Resorts in the World. Toronto, ONT: Pagurian Press, 1976. 191 p. illus. LC 77-362103.

Describes in detail 130 of the most interesting tennis resorts in
the world. Other recreational activities of each resort are also
included. Arranged by country.

305. Zeldin, Dick. A Tennis Guide to the USA. New York: Franklin
Watts, 1980. 216 p. index. LC 80-8.

Arranged alphabetically by city, tennis and racquetball clubs are
listed with descriptions of courts, facilities, prices and locations. Final section identifies hotels with tennis facilities.

ENCYCLOPEDIAS

306. Brady, Maurice. Lawn Tennis Encyclopedia. So. Brunswick, NJ:
A. S. Barnes, 1969. 221 p. illus. LC 71-79755.

Contains 2 major parts: Part I, "Biographies" of 200 past and present players, gives birth date, best world rankings, and highlights
of major tournament records through 1968. For many, a descriptive
paragraph is also included. Part II, "Facts and Figures," lists
winners of major country championships, plus a variety of miscellaneous records.

307. Collins, Bud, and Zander Hollander, eds. Bud Collins' Modern Encyclopedia of Tennis. Garden City, NY: Doubleday, 1980. 389 p.
illus. index. LC 79-8919.

Organized by chronological periods, the history of tennis is traced
from 1876 to present. A round-up of each year's play is provided
starting with the period including 1919. Also has sections on profiles of 50 of the greatest players of all time; brief sketches of
International Tennis Hall of Fame members; and a glossary. Appendixes for rules and records of U. S. championships plus all other
national and international championships.

308. Grimsley, Will. Tennis: Its History, People and Events. Engle-
      wood Cliffs, NJ: Prentice-Hall, 1971. 380 p. illus. index.
      LC 76-144006.

      Exhaustive treatment of the history, players, big events, and con-
      troversies of tennis. Includes sections on tournaments and records
      and "Styles of the Greats." Ends with a long section on "Tennis'
      Most Historic Games" and other miscellany. Many photos.

309. Hedges, Martin. The Concise Dictionary of Tennis. New York: May-
      flower Books, 1978. 278 p. illus. bibl. LC 79-123679.

      In three parts, this contains an alphabetical, lengthy section on
      careers of players from the 1900's to 1978 and entries for asso-
      ciations, tennis-playing countries, courts, tournaments and cham-
      pionships. The glossary section explains terms and rules. Part 3
      is a listing with scores and dates of winners of major tennis
      events.

310. Robertson, Maxwell, and Jack Kramer, eds. The Encyclopedia of Ten-
      nis. New York: Viking, 1974. 392 p. illus. LC 73-10776.

      Having a British emphasis, this source is arranged in 3 sections:
      1. the history and development of tennis, rules, courts and equip-
      ment, and instruction; 2. an alphabetical arrangement of entries
      for individual players, developments in specific countries, terms,
      etc.; 3. tables of records of championships and cup matches.
      Many color plates.

311. Shannon, Bill, ed. United States Tennis Association Official En-
      cyclopedia of Tennis. Rev. and updated ed. New York: Harper
      and Row, 1981. 558 p. illus. index. LC 81-47237.

      Labeled as the "centennial edition," this is the latest revision
      of the 1979 revised edition. It is a vast and comprehensive com-
      pendium organized in 7 sections: history, equipment, principles
      of tennis, rules and etiquette, results of major tournaments and
      championships, tennis greats, and a glossary. The section on ten-
      nis greats has brief sketches of the American Hall of Fame lawn
      tennis players, an alphabetical list of the "World Tennis Roll of
      Honor," yearly USTA and world rankings, plus other all-time records
      and rankings. Subject index does not contain personal names.

STATISTICAL SOURCES

312. The Official U. S. Tennis Association Yearbook and Tennis Guide
      with the Official Rules. Lynn, MA: U. S. Tennis Association.
      Annual. 1937-   . illus. index. ISSN 0083-1557.

The complete compendium of records, calendar of matches, listing
of champions both past and present, career sketches of current season's champions, records and ranking of the various sections in the
U. S. Tennis Assoc., international records, Davis and Wightman Cup
history, and official rules, by-laws and regulations and orders of
USTA. A complete USTA membership roll completes this source. (Formerly entitled the U. S. Lawn Tennis Association Yearbook.) (1980
ed. examined.)

313. Player Records. Princeton, NJ: United States Tennis Association.
     Annual. 1975-1980? ISSN 0363-8766.

     This source provides a detailed record of tournament results for
     leading men and women players for the previous year. Information
     includes dates and names of the tournament, how far the player got,
     who he or she defeated or was defeated by in each round, and the
     prize money won. (Based on 1979 secondary source.)

314. Tennis Annual. Norwalk, CT: Tennis Features. Annual. 1966-   .
     illus.

     Includes features on tennis instruction and the previous season's
     records. The records section is most extensive, with coverage for
     player statistics, tournament results, pro, amateur, jr. champions,
     and all-time records. Brief sketches on players for the current
     season and preview/review of other racquet sports are also included.
     (Based on 1979 secondary source.)

315. United States Squash Racquets Association's Official Yearbook. Bala
     Cynwyd, PA: U. S. Squash Racquets Association. Annual.
     1925-   . ISSN 0083-3398.

     A review of the preceding year is provided including tournament re-
     sults, national rankings, limited international contests, and re-
     sults of national association activities for Canada, Mexico, inter-
     collegiate, and professional. Also includes names and addresses of
     officers, national tournament rules, and current season tournament
     schedules. (Based on 1979 secondary source.)

316. World of Tennis - A BP and Commercial Union Yearbook. Ed. by John
     Barrett. New York: Simon and Schuster. Annual. 1971-   .
     illus. index.

     Produced by the BP International Tennis Fellowship of London, Eng-
     land, this yearbook is a compilation of statistics and career sket-
     ches of international tennis greats. The year's results for nearly
     all international competitions and national tournaments are pro-
     vided, as are historical data for U. S. Cup records and Australian,
     French, British and U. S. Championship Rolls. (1974 ed. examined.)

OTHER

317. Davidson, Owen, and C. M. Jones. Lawn Tennis: The Great Ones.
     The Great Ones Series. London, ENG: Pelham Books, 1970. Distr.
     by Transatlantic Arts, New York. 160 p. illus. LC 70-509027.

Beginning with a chapter tracing the achievements of several out-standing players from 1877 through the early 1920's, this source then devotes a separate chapter to 14 tennis stars. The arrangement is chronological, and intertwined with information about these international all-time greats is the history of tennis up to the late 1960's.

318.   The Tennis Player's Handbook: A Buyer's Guide and Service Direc-tory. By the editors of Tennis Magazine. Norwalk, CT: Tennis Magazine, 1980. 318 p. illus. LC 79-65033.

Composed of numerous brief articles with many diagrams and other illustrations, this source covers such practical topics as choosing proper equipment and clothing; understanding how court surfaces dif-fer; court courtesy; selecting an instructor; common court injuries and how to prevent them; choosing a tennis clinic, etc. Directory of tennis organizations completes this source.

26.
TRACK AND FIELD

BIOGRAPHICAL SOURCES

319. Hanley, Reid M. Who's Who in Track and Field. New Rochelle, NY:
      Arlington House, 1973. 160 p. LC 73-11872.

      Biographies of 420 of the world's greatest athletes and coaches in
      track and field, from 1906 to 1973. Information was gathered from
      athletic organizations throughout the world, as well as from per-
      sonal interviews.

320. Nelson, Cordner. Track and Field - The Great Ones. London, ENG:
      Pelham Books, 1970. Distr. by Tafnews Press, CA. 223 p. illus.
      index. LC 74-504643.

      This source recounts the highlights of the careers of 192 of the
      greatest athletes, with 13 described in considerable detail. Sin-
      gle subject/name index.

321. Nelson, Cordner, and Roberto Quercetani. Runners and Races: The
      1500 M/Mile. Los Altos, CA: Tafnews Press, 1973. 326 p. illus.
      index. LC 72-90579.

      Arranged chronologically, this source intertwines the history of
      particular 1 mile (1500 meter) races with rather brief descriptions
      of individual star runners. Time scope is from 19th century through
      1972. From 1919 and for successive years charts tabulate the year's
      fastest times for the mile and 1500 meters, giving name of runner,
      place, and date of event. "All Time World List" of record times
      completes the book. Name index.

322. Prep Track and Field Athletes of the Year. Montgomery, AL: Coach
      and Athlete. Annual. 19?-   . ISSN 0361-1051.

      Alphabetically arranged biographical sketches of over 3,000 most
      outstanding track and field athletes from high school teams across
      the country. Profile includes name, address, personal data, coach,
      league class and records. (1975 ed. examined.)

ENCYCLOPEDIAS

323. Watman, Melvyn Francis, comp. The Encyclopaedia of Track and Field
      Athletics. 5th ed. New York: St. Martin's Press, 1981. 240 p.
      illus. index. LC 81-52468.

      Basically an A to Z arrangement of 150 biographical sketches, plus
      records of different international, European, Asian, and Common-
      wealth games. Under Olympic Games, names of British medalists come
      first, followed by champions of other events from 1896 to 1980. A
      special feature is a list of athletes cross referenced to the edi-
      tions of the previously published title, Encyclopaedia of Athletics
      in which their biographies appeared. Name index only.

324. Wilt, Fred, and Tom Ecker, eds. International Track and Field
      Coaching Encyclopedia. West Nyack, NY: Parker Pub., 1970.
      350 p. illus. LC 77-87270.

      Arranged into 3 parts: running events, jumping events, and throw-
      ing events, are in-depth discussions of techniques by 23 expert
      coaches from 13 countries. No index.

STATISTICAL SOURCES

325. American Athletics Annual. Indianapolis, IN: Press Information
      Department, The Athletics Congress. Annual. 1980-   .

      Statistics for world records, world junior records, all-time lists,
      rankings, national and international championships, and the year in
      review. Career statistical abstract section details 3,000 athletes'
      performances grouped by events. (1981 ed. examined.)

326. Association of Track and Field Statisticians. Ed. by Donald H.
      Potts. Los Altos, CA: Tafnews Press. Annual. 19?-   . illus.

      Records of winners in events held in 11 different meets, from Bri-
      tish Commonwealth, Europe to Asia and Africa. Also includes infor-
      mation on athletes' nationality, year of birth, meet place and date.
      (1977 ed. examined.)

327. Canadian Interscholastic Track and Field Annual Record Book. Otta-
      wa, ONT: Canadian Federation of Provincial School Athletic Asso-
      ciations. Annual. 19?-   .

      Results of the preceding year's provincial high school track and
      field meets reported by the associations. Includes top ten lists
      for senior, junior, and best times and distances made. In English
      and French. (1980 ed. examined.)

328. Ganslen, R. V. Mechanics of the Pole Vault. 1980 Olympic 9th ed.
      Denton, TX: Ganslen, 1979. 176 p. illus. bibl. LC 80-80295.

Basically a manual on training, psychology, and mechanics, interspersed with drawings, photographic sequences and computer trace of
vault flight. Survey of 21 world vaulters reveals their techniques.
The last section presents in fine print a 100 year statistical history, including outstanding performers by decade.

329. High School Track. Los Altos, CA: Tafnews Press. Annual.
     196?-   . illus.

A record of high school track for the preceding year. Winning marks
and some non-winning marks from any authorized competition are recorded. Includes brief notes on athletes of the year. (1979 ed.
examined.)

330. Indoor Track With Records, All-Time and 1970 World Lists. By edi-
     torial staff of Track and Field News. Los Altos, CA: Tafnews
     Press, 1970. 48 p. illus. LC 71-28972.

Statistics on world bests, European bests, and American and world
all-time and 1970 world indoor track competitions. Includes biographies of five outstanding athletes and a directory of track facilities by countries and cities.

331. Luther, Walter, ed. The Masters of Track and Field. Toronto, ONT:
     Colban of Canada, 1975. 95 p. illus. LC 79-318385.

The only reference feature of this book is the charts of world masters' records in 3 age groups from 40 to 70. The rest of the book
introduces the winners through essays and photos. No index.

332. Marathon Handbook. By the editors of Runner's World. Mountain
     View, CA: World Publications. Annual. 1970?-   . illus.
     ISSN 0360-9928.

This annual has evolved to include sections on world-wide, all-time
marathon records; U. S. and Canadian male and female records by time
and age; a yearly marathon calendar of races; listing and records
for other races (15 kilometers, etc.); listing and records for race
walking; and a section on records for the 24 hour relay. (Based on
1978 secondary source.)

333. Martin, D. E. and R. W. Gynn. Marathon Footrace: Performers and
     Performances. Springfield, IL: Charles C. Thomas, 1979. 469 p.
     illus. bibl. index. LC 79-1035.

A definitive and scholarly work on the history of the marathon, complete with statistics for major regional and local races. Included
in the appendixes are profiles of top marathon runners, statistics
on progression of world fastest performers, and chronological listings for men and women performances of sub-2:20. Bibliography and
name and subject indexes complete the volume.

334. Mundle, Peter, and Katharine Brieger, comps. Masters Age Records.
     Los Altos, CA: Tafnews Press, 1979. 54 p.

Age and performance records for 44 events of men and women participants for age 35 and above. Also has information on residence, date
of birth, site and date of meets.

335. NAGWS Guide - Track and Field. Reston, VA: American Alliance for
Health, Physical Education, Recreation and Dance. National Asso-
ciation for Girls and Women in Sport. Biennial. 1962/64-   .
ISSN 0362-9481.

After the first two sections on standards, committee directory and
rules, comes the major portion which provides team competition
championship results for the past 10 years and women's indoor, outdoor, and junior college records. Other features include: glossary, scoring tables, officiating principles and techniques. (Continues Track and Field Guide with Official Rules and Standards,
1962/64-1973/75, which superseded in part Softball, Track and Field
Guide.) (1981-82 ed. examined.)

336. NCAA Track and Field. Shawnee Mission, KS: National Collegiate
Athletic Association. Annual. 1922-   . ISSN 0277-6677.

A record book of various collegiate track and field championships
of the year, arranged by divisions, regional conferences, indoor,
cross-country, etc. Official world records are given. A section
on rules indicates major rules changes for the year. (Formerly
Official National Collegiate Athletic Association Track and Field
Guide, 1922-1979, ISSN 0196-9358.) (1981 ed. examined.)

337. Official AAU Track and Field Handbook. Indianapolis, IN: Amateur
Athletic Union of the United States. Biennial. 1942-   . ISSN
0361-347X.

World, national, and U. S. championship records. Also includes
equipment specifications. (Combines AAU Official Track and Field
Handbook, Rules and Records, 196?-1973/74 and AAU Official Track
and Field Handbook, 1942-74.) (Based on 1982 secondary source.)

338. Olympic Track and Field. By the editors of Track and Field News.
Los Altos, CA: Tafnews Press, 1979. 192 p. illus. LC 79-
121020.

Record book of the Summer Olympics from 1896 to 1976. Includes
brief notes on the events with separate sections for men and women.
A special feature is a section on Olympic trivia of unusual achievements and incidents. Complete title is Olympic Track and Field:
Complete Men's and Women's Olympic Track and Field Results, 1896-
1976, Plus a Wealth of Other Olympic Esoterica.

339. Shepard, Jack, Wally Donovan, and Peter Mundle, comps. Age Records;
World, United States Bests, Track and Field... Los Altos, CA:
Tafnews Press, 1975. LC 76-359499.

A record of marks as of January, 1975 for 47 events in track and field from ages 0 - 89. Information includes age, marks, athletes' names, residence, and year of event. Marks included must be recorded in legitimate competitions. The shortest event record is the 50 yd. dash. Complete title is Age Records: World, United States Bests, Track and Field, Ages 0 to 89 Included as of January 1, 1975, Based on Actual Birthdates: 47 Events Listed, English Metric Measurements.

340. Visek, Vladimir, comp. Top Ten Averages. Los Altos, CA: Tafnews Press, 1972. 102 p.

Statistics and rankings of athletes by the averages of their best ten marks. For every event, 50 athletes are included in rank order, each with a list of the ten marks, place and date of events. No index.

OTHER

341. Morrison, Ray Leon. An Annotated Bibliography of Track and Field Books Published in the United States Between 1960-1974. San Jose, CA: San Jose State University, 1975. 115 p. (ERIC ED 147 271).

The author's masters thesis is this annotated list of all books, including juvenile literature, located by the author at Track and Field News Inc. and World Publications. Subject matter ranges from running events, field events, biographies, and statistics, with imprint dates between 1960 and 1974. Titles are arranged under broad subject headings, then alphabetically. A separate section lists periodicals and publishers. There are indexes for author, title, publishers and magazines.

27.
VOLLEYBALL

342. Annual Official Volleyball Reference Guide of the United States
     Volleyball Association. Colorado Springs, CO: United States
     Volleyball Association. Annual. 1917-   . illus. ISSN 0083-
     3592.

     Arranged in 4 sections with a detailed table of contents, this
     guide provides much directory-type information for the officers and
     directors of the national association, as well as the officials for
     each of the 29 regions. Other noteworthy parts are the career
     sketches of various award recipients; the results of a variety of
     championships; the bibliography of books, films, and magazines;
     listing of volleyball archives; and the final section on refereeing,
     scoring, conducting tournaments, and the official rules. (1981 ed.
     examined.)

343. NAGWS Guide - Volleyball. Reston, VA: American Alliance for
     Health, Physical Education, Recreation and Dance. National Asso-
     ciation for Girls and Women in Sport. Biennial. 1938-   .
     illus. ISSN 0145-1987.

     Primarily this guide provides commentary and explanation for the of-
     ficial rules. Also includes court/game protocol, information on of-
     ficiating, list of national officials, and a final section on the
     AIAW Championship results and the NAIA and NJCAA Women's Champion-
     ship results. (Formerly Volleyball Guide.) (1982/83 ed. examined.)

344. Ross, Saul. Volleyball Bibliography. Ottawa, ONT: Canadian Vol-
     leyball Association, 1973. (11 p. unpaged).

     This bibliography groups and lists material by type of publication.
     Includes books, journal articles, films, and filmstrips.

28.
WATER POLO

345. Cutino, Peter J., and Dennis R. Bledsoe. <u>Polo: The Manual for
Coach and Player</u>. Los Angeles, CA: Swimming World Pub., 1976.
179 p. illus. index. LC 75-20710.

A useful reference manual on the techniques, conditioning and play
strategies. Terms are grouped into chapters on passing, shooting,
individual defense, goalie play, etc. and illustrated with line
drawings and photos. The last chapter contains suggestions and
opinions from 18 members of various championship teams, describing
their best moves and other aspects of the game. The appendix provides a complete step by step example of various drills, style and
system of play at U. C. Berkeley where Cutino is the head coach.
Subject index.

346. Somali, Ivan V. <u>A Bibliography of Water Polo 1901-1973</u>. Ottawa,
ONT: Canadian Water Polo Association Inc., Division of the Ca-
nadian Federation of Amateur Aquatics Inc. (unpaged). index.
(SIRC GV 839 .W3 #58).

An in-house publication of approximately 100 titles of books, rules,
manuals, periodical articles, and audio-visual materials organized
into 6 separate sections. Most are available from the author's
collection. Includes an index of publishers and distributors.

29.
WRESTLING

ENCYCLOPEDIAS

347. Carson, Ray. Encyclopedia of Championship Wrestling Drills. Cran-
bury, NJ: A. S. Barnes, 1974. 144 p. bibl. LC 73-18862.

One hundred and one drills grouped into six categories from rota-
tional and competitional to recreational, etc. Each move is illustrated with diagrams and photos. The principles of each type
of drill are explained. Without an index, the use of this book
requires a knowledge of what category a particular drill falls into.

348. Clayton, Thompson, comp. A Handbook of Wrestling Terms and Holds.
New and rev. ed. So. Brunswick, NJ: A. S. Barnes, 1974. 192 p.
illus. bibl. index. LC 74-168291.

Fully illustrated book on wrestling maneuvers. Terms of the same
moves are grouped under the most popular ones. Index provides the
only means of access.

349. Jesse, John. Wrestling Physical Conditioning Encyclopedia. Pasa-
dena, CA: The Athletic Press, 1974. 416 p. illus. bibl. index. LC 74-5197.

More like a handbook than an encyclopedia, this source explains the
why, how and when of physical conditioning for wrestlers with emphasis on principles and muscle anatomy. Includes caloric chart
and subject index.

OTHER

350. NCAA Wrestling. Shawnee Mission, KS: National Collegiate Athletic
Association. Annual. 1928-   . illus. index.

This guide provides the current year's roundups and past year's records grouped into divisions and conferences. Official rules section includes rule changes, hand signals, high school differences and coaches code of ethics. There is an index to rules. (Continues Official National Collegiate Athletic Association Wrestling Guide, 1928-1979.) (1982 ed. examined.)

351. Official AAU Wrestling Rule/Handbook. Lincoln, NB: Amateur Athletic Union of the United States, Wrestling Division. Annual. 19?-   . illus.

This handbook contains official rules and past season's records. It also includes information for officials and requirements for participation in international games. (Formerly Official AAU Wrestling Handbook, 19?-1979.) (Based on 1980 secondary source.)

352. Ross, S. Wrestling Bibliography. Ottawa, ONT: University of Ottawa, Center of Sport Studies, 1973. (unpaged). (SIRC GV 1195 #2760).

This in-house bibliography lists approximately 60 titles of books, articles, films, media on wrestling published between 1939-1970.

PART II
SPORTS AND PHYSICAL EDUCATION: GENERAL AND TOPICAL

30.
SPORTS AND PHYSICAL
EDUCATION: GENERAL

BIBLIOGRAPHICAL SOURCES
ELEMENTARY/SECONDARY SCHOOL MATERIALS

353. Advisory List of Instructional Media for Health, Safety, and Physi-
      cal Education. Raleigh, NC: North Carolina State Dept. of Pub-
      lic Instruction, 1977. 45 p. (ERIC ED 149 748).

      Listed by type of media are books, films, filmstrips, kits, record-
      ings, and study prints ranging from primary to senior high school
      grade levels. Suitable for physical education, health and safety
      programs.

354. Blickle, Calvin, and Francis Corcoran. Sports: A Multimedia Guide
      for Children and Young Adults. Selection Guide Series, No. 6.
      New York: Neal-Schuman Pub.; Santa Barbara, CA: ABC-Clio, 1980.
      245 p. index. LC 80-13519.

      Annotated selection guide to building an up-to-date core collection
      in sports for elementary and secondary grades. Includes over 500
      titles of printed and audiovisual materials. Nine separate indexes
      and a directory of publishers and producers.

355. Duncan, Armstrong, and Heather Wilson, comps. An Annotated Cata-
      logue of Research Relating to Children and Physical Activity.
      Vanier, ONT: Canadian Association for Health, Physical Education
      and Recreation, 1980. 149 p. index.

      An annotated bibliography organized into the following sections:
      general fitness and health, physiological reports relating to chil-
      dren, curriculum theory for physical education, motor learning and
      child development, sports psychology and its application to chil-
      dren, children and sport, sports medicine, children and recreation,
      and physical education and atypical children. The annotations are
      extremely thorough, often providing results of research findings.
      Journals, unpublished reports and theses are included. Journal
      and author indexes.

356. Harrah, Barbara K. Sports Books for Children: An Annotated Bib-
      liography. Metuchen, NJ: Scarecrow, 1978. 526 p. index. LC
      78-18510.

      Arranged by categories of sports and then subdivided, the 3,059 ti-
      tles cover a wide range of sports of interest to preschool - grade
      12. Interest and/or readability level indicated in citation. Has
      a periodical list and author and title indexes.

357. Library of Congress. Division for the Blind and Physically Handi-
      capped. Sports - A Selected List of Books That Have Appeared in
      Talking Book Topics and Braille Book Review. Washington, DC:
      Government Printing Office, 1977. 56 p. LC 77-13139. (SUDOC
      LC 19.11 Sp6).

      Arranged by sport, and then by disc, cassette, and braille, this
      source lists and annotates books that are available for the blind.
      Narrators' names are provided, as are the indication of interest
      level and category of fiction or non-fiction. Three indexes ar-
      ranged by author, for cassette, braille, and disc media. A disc
      of the bibliography accompanies it.

358. Manitoba Physical Education and Recreation Instructional Media.
      Winnipeg, Manitoba: Manitoba Department of Education, 1980.
      55 p. (ERIC ED 198 083).

      Lists and provides location information for books, cassettes,
      slides, kits, super 8 film loops, records and 16 mm films on various
      sports. Educational support services identified and explained.

359. New Perspectives for Elementary School Physical Education Programs
      in Canada: Catalogue of Resources. Ottawa, ONT: Canadian Asso-
      ciation for Health, Physical Education and Recreation, 1979.
      106 p.

      Arranged by subject categories with type of document sub-headings,
      this resources guide lists and annotates the provincial, regional,
      and local program guides, related literature, research studies, pa-
      pers and curriculum guides relating to elementary school physical
      education in Canada, U. S. and some European countries.

360. Ritzzitiello, Theresa G. An Annotated Bibliography on Movement Edu-
      cation for the Elementary School Physical Education Council.
      Washington, DC: National Association for Sport and Physical Edu-
      cation. American Alliance for Health, Physical Education and Re-
      creation, 1977. 49 p. index. LC 77-373216. (ERIC ED 144 936).

      Annotated list of monographs organized into a theory section and a
      practice section. Titles are further divided into those for basic
      movement, dance - drama, gymnastics, and sports. Emphasis is placed
      on child development. Author and titles interfile into one alpha-
      betical index. Publications range from 1963 to 1975.

FACILITIES

361. Beard, James B., et al. Turfgrass Bibliography from 1672 to 1972.
      E. Lansing, MI: Michigan State University Press, 1977. 730 p.
      index. LC 75-21100.

      Truly the most extensive bibliography available of international
      literature on the science and culture of turfgrass. Over 16,000
      entries to books, periodical literature, conference proceedings,
      and obscure state and regional trade/specialized publications are
      arranged alphabetically by main entry. A 161 page subject index
      allows for specific subject access. Although the primary audience
      is for private and commercial turfgrass researchers and practicing
      professionals, the sports manager would also find this useful.

362. Coppa and Avery Consultants. Physical Education Facilities: Plan-
      ning the Facility, Sound Absorption, Playing Surfaces, Physical
      Education and the Handicapped, and Pool Design. Architecture
      Series: Bibliography # A267. Monticello, IL: Vance Bibliogra-
      phies, 1980. 9 p. LC 80-126193.

      Provides the reader with titles published from 1959 to 1976 on the
      design of physical education facilities, grouped into sound absorp-
      tion, playing surfaces, etc.

363. Starbuck, James C. Stadiums: A Bibliography. Exchange Bibliogra-
      phy #681. Monticello, IL: Council of Planning Librarians, 1974.
      24 p. LC 75-314185.

      This source includes articles from 71 periodicals, ranging from
      popular sports, to architecture, to engineering periodicals. En-
      tries are alphabetical by periodical, with articles chronologically
      arranged within each.

PHYSICAL EDUCATION AND SPORTS

364. Abstracts of Research Papers. Reston, VA: American Alliance for
        Health, Physical Education, Recreation and Dance. Annual.
        1968-   . index. ISSN 0587-4890.

        As indicated by its title, this contains abstracts of papers ac-
        cepted for presentation at the AAHPERD annual convention. Arranged
        chronologically by the date and time the papers were presented,
        with an author index. (1982 ed. examined).

365. Donahee, Gary R. Sports Bibliography. Ottawa, ONT: Coaching As-
        sociation of Canada, 1973? 130 p.

        Predecessor to the current Sport Bibliography (#366), this lists
        books, theses, etc. under sport categories. Time scope covers
        early 1940's through 1970-71. English language materials only.

366. Draayer, I., et al., eds. Sport Bibliography/Bibliographie du
        Sport. 8 vols. Ottawa, ONT: Sport Information Resource Center,
        1981. index. LC 81-123029.

        A comprehensive, computer-generated, English - French bibliography
        of some 70,000 citations on all subjects related to physical ac-
        tivity and sports for the period 1974-1980. (Substantial, but less
        complete coverage prior to 1974.) Provides subject access to peri-
        odical articles, books, theses, conference proceedings, pamphlets,
        and unpublished materials. The first four volumes deal with spe-
        cific sports, while the following four volumes cover such allied
        fields as sports medicine, history of sport, coaching, psychology
        of sport, handicapped and sport, etc. Each volume has a detailed
        table of contents and a subject index so that the numerous subdi-
        visions of the subject headings are quickly accessible. Titles of
        foreign language publications are translated into English. Annual
        updates are planned beginning with the fall of 1982. This 8 vol.
        set can serve as a cumulation for SIRC's monthly periodical index
        Sport and Recreation Index (#556) for the time period covered.

367. Educator's Guide to Free Health, Physical Education and Recreation
      Materials. Ed. by Foley A. Horkheimer. Randolph, WI: Educators
      Progress Service, Inc. Annual. 1968-   . index.

      This catalog annotates and identifies free materials by media types,
      such as films, filmstrips, slides, tapes and printed publications,
      and then categorizes these into health, physical education and re-
      creation-related. Title, subject, source availability and Canadian
      availability indexes. (1981 ed. examined.)

368. Eshelby, Don, comp. Physical Education: A Bibliography of Select-
      ed Documents from ERIC. Grand Forks, ND: North Dakota Univer-
      sity, 1970. 16 p. (ERIC ED 043 405).

      More than 100 citations are listed by main entry in alphabetical
      order in the three sections "Physical Education," "Physical Educa-
      tion Facilities," and "Physical Fitness." These citations were
      taken from 1967, 1968, and 1969 volumes of Research in Education.
      No annotations and no indexes.

369. Eyler, Marvin. A Selected Annotated Bibliography on Physical Edu-
      cation. Washington, DC: ERIC Clearinghouse on Teacher Educa-
      tion, 1974. 72 p. (ERIC ED 090 143).

      Alphabetically arranged by author in an ERIC documents section and
      a journal citations section, this annotated bibliography covers the
      years 1966-1973.

370. Fonger, Sandra, et al. The Compilation of a Selected Bibliography
      of Relevant Theses and Research in International Comparative Phy-
      sical Education and Sport in the U. S. A. and Canada. 1972.
      14 p. (ERIC ED 115 611).

      This source lists 187 research publications from 1930 to 1972, or-
      ganized into masters theses, doctoral dissertations and miscella-
      neous sections.

371. Health, Physical Education, and Recreation Microform Publications
      Bulletin. Eugene, OR: University of Oregon, School of Health,
      Physical Education, and Recreation. Irregular. 1964-   .
      ISSN 0090-5119.

      This source is composed of three parts -- citations, subject, and
      author indexes to unpublished doctoral dissertations, masters' the-
      ses, out-of-print journals and books available in the school's mi-
      croform collection. Citations, grouped into broad subject areas,
      are arranged alphabetically by author. (Formerly known as Health,
      Physical Education and Recreation Microcard Bulletin, 1964-1972,
      ISSN 0017-906X.) (1972 ed. examined.)

372. Herndon, Myrtis E., comp. Comparative Physical Education and Inter-
      national Sport. 2 vols. Washington, DC: American Allicance for
      Health, Physical Education and Recreation, 1972. index. LC 72-
      196004.

Some 6,000 books, articles and theses on the subject are included. Volume 1, "A Bibliographic Guide," concentrates on comparative physical education, international sport and dance, with a country index for each section. Volume 2, "A Bibliographic Guide to the Asian Countries," deals with sports in Asian countries, with entries arranged by regions and countries, and a single name-subject index.

373. Illinois University at Urbana - Champaign. Applied Life Studies Library. Dictionary Catalog of the Applied Life Studies Library. 4 vol. Boston, MA: G. K. Hall, 1977. LC 77-360766.

A dictionary catalog of the Applied Life Studies Library's collection of over 17,000 books, microfilms, pamphlets, etc. Subject coverage includes physical education and allied fields, outdoor recreation, health and safety education, and dance. Each page of the catalog reproduces 21 title cards in miniature size, complete with Dewey numbers used by the library and organized by Library of Congress subject headings. First supplement of 2 volumes has been published in 1982 by G. K. Hall.

374. McGuire, Raymond, and Pat Mueller. Bibliography of References for Intramurals and Recreational Sports. Cornwall, NY: Leisure Press, 1975. 91 p. index. LC 79-127170. (ERIC ED 129 825).

Over 1,500 entries for articles dealing with intramural and leisure programs are arranged alphabetically by author. Subject index precedes the main section. Coverage ranges from early 1900 to 1975.

375. Nueckel, Susan. Selected Guide to Sports and Recreation Books. New York: Fleet Press Corp., 1974. 168 p. index. LC 73-3735.

Materials are listed alphabetically with one sentence "annotations" in 70 different categories of sports, recreational activities, and hobbies. Directory of publishers included.

376. Nunn, Marshall E. Sports. Spare Time Guides Series, No. 10. Littleton, CO: Libraries Unlimited, 1976. 217 p. index. LC 75-33869.

A classified annotated bibliography of 649 books on major competitive U. S. sports that were in-print in early 1975. Within each chapter there are sections for reference and non-reference titles. Also included are an annotated listing of 93 sports periodicals, a list of associations, and a directory of publishers.

377. Ontario. Sports and Recreation Bureau. Audio-Visual Catalogue. Toronto, ONT: Sports and Recreation Bureau, 1975. 55 p. index. LC 77-355800.

378. Reed, James Lee. A Compendium of Selected Theses on Intramural Programs. Masters Thesis. University of Illinois, 1971. Eugene, OR: University of Oregon, School of Health, Physical Education and Recreation. Microform Publications, 1973. 177 p. index.

Microfiche of the author's masters thesis completed at the University of Illinois, Urbana - Champaign in 1971. Basically, this is an updated list of masters theses and Ph.D. dissertations found in Raymond James McGuire's 1966 masters thesis on intramural research. Annotations all organized into 16 specific areas of concentration, such as philosophy and history, finance, objectives, etc. Author index.

379. Reed, Maxine K., ed. The Videotape/Disc Guide: Sports and Recreation. Syosset, NY: National Video Clearinghouse Inc., 1980. 83 p. illus. index.

Lists videotapes and videocassettes alphabetically by title. Each entry provides the following information: title, producer, date of release, running time, color/black and white, video formats available, suitability of use (e.g., for home use, school use, etc.), age of target audience, availability for rental or purchase, and a summary of the program. When relevant, other information is provided, such as notes about ancilliary materials, captions for hearing impaired, etc. Subject index allows access by sport.

380. Turner, Pearl, comp. Index to Outdoor Sports, Games and Activities. Useful Reference Series, No. 105. Westwood, MA: F. W. Faxon, 1978. 409 p. LC 77-72795.

This source provides access to how-to books and articles on 92 outdoor competitive and non-competitive sports for the period 1970 through 1975. There is a list of individual sports and games terms, followed by a list of abbreviations used for books indexed. The main section follows in which entries are arranged under sports. Most titles are tagged with a keyword to identify their intended age group or sex. The last section is a list of all books indexed, grouped by sport.

BIOGRAPHICAL SOURCES

381. Batten, Jack. Champions. Toronto, ONT: Newpress, 1971. 197 p.
      illus. index. LC 72-181757.

      Illustrative history of Canadian sports focusing on the famous
      players, with records for hockey, curling and football champions.
      Player index. Arranged by individual sport.

382. Darden, Anne. The Sports Hall of Fame. New York: Drake Pub.,
      1976. 236 p. illus. LC 76-28312.

      Very brief summaries of the careers and records of outstanding ath-
      letes in 14 sports. Baseball, with 20 biographical sketches, has
      the most of all the sports included. Each sketch is followed by a
      full-page, black and white photograph.

383. Famous American Athletes of Today. 10 vols. 1932-1938; reprint.
      Essay Index Reprint Series. Freeport, NY: Books for Libraries
      Press, 1971. LC 70-93348.

      Originally published as part of the Famous Leaders Series, 1932-
      1938, these volumes have been reprinted, and series 3 - 5 have been
      revised. Each volume contains about 15 lengthy biographies of fa-
      mous athletes of the period. Most of the volumes have a different
      author(s).

384. Ferguson, Bob. Who's Who in Canadian Sport. Scarborough, ONT:
      Prentice Hall of Canada, 1977. 310 p. LC 77-378486.

      In an A - Z format, brief sketches of over 1,300 Canadian athletes
      and sports figures are included. Listing in back groups persons
      included by sport.

385. Grimsley, Will, ed. The Sports Immortals. Englewood Cliffs, NJ:
      Prentice-Hall, 1972. 320 p. illus. LC 72-6900.

This book makes an effort to capture the spirit of each era in the 20th century up through 1950 by representing each sport with the athletes "who cast the largest shadows." Associated Press reporters selected the 50 sports stars, and each entry includes a brief history of the athlete's time period along with the biography.

386. Hickok, Ralph. Who Was Who in American Sports. New York: Hawthorn Books, 1971. 338 p. illus. index. LC 72-158009.

Biographical sketches of approximately 1,500 American sports figures in 42 sports. Baseball and football personalities comprise 58% of the sketches. Includes an index of personalities by sport.

387. Keylin, Arleen, and J. Cohen, eds. The New York Times Sports Hall of Fame. New York: Arno Press, 1981. 184 p. illus. bibl. LC 80-28594.

Obituaries from the New York Times for 92 sports heroes from late 1800's to the present. Alphabetically arranged by name.

388. The Lincoln Library of Sports Champions. 20 vols. 3rd ed. Columbus, OH: Frontier Press, 1981. illus. bibl. index. LC 80-54174.

Although this set is designed for students, it is useful for sports novices of any age. From archery to wrestling, 2 to 3 page biographical sketches with numerous photographs are arranged alphabetically by athlete for more than 500 sports champions, past and present. A glossary and master name index are in vol. 20.

389. Litsky, Frank. Superstars. Secaucus, NJ: Derbibooks, Inc., 1975. 352 p. illus. LC 75-7753.

One-page overviews for 280 famous sports figures written by a well known sports journalist. Photos accompany each figure. Biographical particulars and records are not included in entries; instead, one finds an overall description of the personality and/or achievements that are responsible for the biographee's excellence.

390. Pachter, Marc. Champions of American Sport. New York: H. N. Abrams, 1981. 288 p. illux. LC 80-28934.

Catalog of the exhibition "Champions of Sport" held at the National Portrait Gallery, Smithsonian Museum, June 23 - September 7, 1981. Covering a range of time periods and sports from baseball to yachting (even rodeo), this catalog spotlights 100 sports heroes and documents the first major sports exhibition ever mounted in the U. S. Biographies are about a page each, but the photographs and reproductions of artistic works compose the major part of this source.

391. Willoughby, David P. The Super-Athletes. So. Brunswick, NJ: A. S. Barnes, 1970. 665 p. illus. bibl. index. LC 72-88302.

Organized in 3 broad categories of "Feats of Strength," "Field Athletics," and "Women Athletes" with many sections for specific acts
of strength/endurance and sports, this source documents the "best"
performances of physical strength by tracing historically the records made by both amateur and professional athletes and non-ath-
letes who hold a world or national record. There are biographical
sketches interspersed with descriptions of record-makers. Section
on women athletes is small and of poor quality. Many photos. Name
index provides the only easy access to persons included.

392. Wise, Sydney F., and Douglas Fisher. <u>Canada's Sporting Heroes.</u>
     Don Mills, ONT: General Publishing Co., 1974. 338 p. illus.
     bibl. index. LC 75-302812.

Biographies of members of Canada's Sports Hall of Fame. Descriptions are grouped by sports with a preface on the history for each
section. Includes an extensive bibliography and index of names and
subjects.

DICTIONARIES/ENCYCLOPEDIAS

Although many of these encyclopedias also include definitions of sports terms or include brief glossaries, they have all been grouped together, except for the first two titles which are strictly dictionaries.

DICTIONARIES

393. Frommer, Harvey. Sports Lingo: A Dictionary of the Language of Sports. New York: Atheneum, 1979. 302 p. index. LC 78-12130.

Arranged by sport, terms, slang, and expressions and their explanations are provided for 40 sports. Focus is on the modern usage and meanings of the terms.

394. Webster's Sports Dictionary. Springfield, MA: G. & C. Merriam Co., 1976. 503 p. illus. LC 75-42076.

Definitions of terms used by players, sportswriters, and broadcasters. Includes idioms of Australian, British and Canadian usage. Different meanings of the same terms are defined under subdivisions by the names of sports. An important feature is the specifications for playing areas and game equipment. Appendix includes abbreviations, referee signals and scorekeeping.

ENCYCLOPEDIAS

395. Anderson, Bob. Sportsource. Mountain View, CA: World Publications, 1975. 430 p. illus. bibl. LC 75-16003.

A handy source because of its introductory coverage of all kinds of sports, including unusual activities like abalone diving, log rolling, frog jumping, etc. Readers are referred to the names of organizations, magazines and books for further information.

396. Arlott, John, ed. The Oxford Companion to Sports and Games. New
      York: Oxford University Press, 1975. 1143 p. illus. LC 75-
      319716.

      Alphabetically arranged with sufficient cross references, this
      source includes most all sports and games which are the subject of
      national or international competition, as well as entries for peo-
      ple, teams, etc. Excluded are "blood sports" (although bull-fight-
      ing is included) and board and table games. Each entry includes a
      description of how the sport is played, its development, structure
      techniques, traditions, and great personalities. Brief bibliogra-
      phies are provided for most sports. Strongly British -- e.g., 52
      pages for "association football" and only 5 for "baseball."

397. Bass, Howard. International Encyclopaedia of Winter Sports. Cran-
      bury, NJ: Great Albion Books, 1972. 224 p. illus. LC 79-37616.

      Alphabetically arranged by winter sport, each chapter describes the
      sport and its most famous champions. Separate sections cover bio-
      graphical sketches of the "top 20" and list of world champions up
      through 1970.

398. Benagh, Jim, and Otto Penzler. ABC's Wide World of Sports Encyclo-
      pedia. New York: Stadia Sports Pub., 1973. 224 p. illus. in-
      dex. LC 73-80406.

      Very brief treatment of the background, stars of the 1970's, and
      historical points for the sports covered on the television program
      "ABC's Wide World of Sports." Auto racing, boxing, figure skating,
      gymnastics, track and field, and swimming have more space devoted
      to them than other sports. Unusual recreational sports events in-
      cluded are: barrel jumping, cliff diving, demolition derby, inter-
      ceptor rocketry, and wrist wrestling. A final section devotes 1 -
      2 pages of biographical information on Wide World's Athletes of the
      Year for the years 1962-1972. Numerous black and white photos.

399. Burton, Bill, ed. The Sportsman's Encyclopedia. New York: Grosset
      and Dunlap, 1971. 638 p. illus. LC 75-26735.

      Lengthy treatment of equipment, technique and rules of 34 sports.
      Each article is accompanied by a glossary of terms.

400. Cuddon, J. A. The International Dictionary of Sports and Games.
      New York: Schocken Books, 1980. 870 p. illus. LC 79-20283.

      Useful for its explanations of lesser-known sports and games, par-
      ticularly British and continental sports and games, this encyclo-
      pedia is quite comprehensive. Entries range in length from 25 pages
      for "Cricket" to 6 lines for the "Dallas Cowboys." In one alpha-
      betical arrangement are place names, equipment, sports, teams, etc.
      Personal names are included only within other entries. No index,
      but sufficient use of cross references.

401. Cureton, Thomas K., Jr., series ed. Encyclopedia of Physical Edu-
      cation and Sports. 5 vols. (projected). 1977-   . LC 76-46608.

Sponsored by the American Alliance for Health, Physical Education, Recreation, and Dance, this series is to include 5 volumes. Currently available are:

Vol. 1 Sports, Dance, and Related Activities. Ed. by Reuben B. Frost. Reading, MA: Addison-Wesley, 1977. 973 p. illus. index.

Vol. 2 Training, Environment, Nutrition, and Fitness. Ed. by G. Alan Stull. Salt Lake City, UT: Brighton Pub. Co., 1980. 614 p. illus. index.

Vol. 3 Philosophy, Programs, and History. Ed. by James S. Bosco and Mary Ann Turner. Salt Lake City, UT: Brighton Pub. Co., 1981. 712 p. illus. bibl. index.

The first 2 volumes were examined. Articles are written by different authors/educators, and some inconsistency of style can be noted. Emphasis in volume one, as opposed to Menke (#407), or Oxford (#396), is on pedagogy, technique, and recent developments in the sports. All articles are followed by selected references. Secondary sources state that volume 3 contains 120 articles, many being old reprints. However, the coverage for physical education for the handicapped spans 200 pages, and an extensive listing of organizations relevant to physical education is included.

402. The Encyclopedia of Sport. 2 vols. Edited by the Earl of Suffolk and B. H. Peek. 1897; reprint. Detroit, MI: Gale, 1976. illus. index. LC 75-23210.

Lengthy, signed articles with bibliographies at the end make up this reprint of the 1897 British publication. All types of sports, including competitive and animal sports, are represented. Even includes briefer, descriptive articles on animals that are of interest to sportsmen, e.g., Theodore Roosevelt wrote the article on caribou.

403. Frommer, Harvey. Sports Roots - How Nicknames, Namesakes, Trophies, Competitions, and Expressions in the World of Sports Came to Be. New York: Atheneum, 1979. 191 p. illus. index. LC 79-9729.

In an A - Z format this unique source explains the origin and significance of many sports, sports personalities' nicknames and quotes, competitions, trophies, and important events. Where else could you find the older, more picturesque names for golfing irons or who first said, "It's not how you win or lose, but how you play the game"?

404. Hickok, Ralph. New Encyclopedia of Sports. New York: McGraw-Hill, 1977. 543 p. illus. LC 76-45633.

Alphabetically arranged, this contains entries for "all North American competitive sports"; historical articles on topics such as "Black Athletes" and "Amateurism"; and other short entries on specialized subjects, such as the implements of fencing. All table games are excluded, but most animal sports and "blood sports" (except bull fighting) are included. Entries for sports include a history, summary of rules, list of results and rewards, and for many sports, biographical section and a glossary. No index, but many

cross references and brief bibliographies, many more illustrations
than Menke (#407) or Oxford (#396), but most libraries don't need
all three. Hickok's coverage of history may be sketchier than the
other two sources, but his frequent discussions of technique and selective glossaries are unique.

405. Hollander, Zander, ed. The Encyclopedia of Sports Talk. New York:
        Corwin Books, 1976. 276 p. illus. LC 76-19253.

Definitions of over 3,500 slang and idioms related to fifteen
sports. Also includes biographies, rules, history and traditions.
Terms are arranged under individual sport chapters, each contributed by professionals in the field. A brief biography of the
contributors precedes the main section. No index.

406. Hovis, Ford, ed. The Sports Encyclopedia. New York: Praeger,
        1976. 224 p. illus. LC 76-21340.

In a rather sketchy manner are approximately 5 - 10 page articles
which summarize the history, equipment, technique, and competitions
for about 60 sports. Alphabetically arranged. Many photos.

407. Menke, Frank G. The Encyclopedia of Sports. 6th rev. ed. Revi-
        sions by Pete Palmer. So. Brunswick, NJ: A. S. Barnes, 1977.
        1132 p. illus. index. LC 76-58581.

Also available in paperback from Doubleday, this source is particularly strong for its coverage of the history of nearly 80 sports.
Along with the Oxford Companion to Sports and Games (#396) and
Hickok (#404) these sources are often considered the best sports
encyclopedias for background and history. Typically the articles
for each sport begin with a history, followed by famous players,
then outstanding all-time records. Articles range from 3 pages to
over 100. The A - Z arrangement includes brief articles on some
associations, but because some of this information is included under "Miscellaneous," one must use the subject index. The only
board games included are chess and checkers. "Blood sports" are
excluded, but some animal sports are included, e.g. dog racing.
Only a few line drawings.

408. Newman, Gerald, ed. The Concise Encyclopedia of Sports. 2nd rev.
        ed. New York: Franklin Watts, 1979. 218 p. illus. index.
        LC 79-10260.

Perhaps more appropriate for the novice, this source includes in
one alphabetical arrangement people, events, and about 85 sports
which are covered in varying detail. Although the depth and comprehensiveness of Menke (#407) is lacking, this source covers more
sports and is profusely illustrated with charts, diagrams and photographs. Excludes all blood sports and all board games. This is
a revision of the 1970 ed. by K. W. Jennison.

409. Spectators Guide to Sports. New York: New American Library, 1976.
        192 p. illus. LC 75-39883.

Designed as a reference guide for spectators, this source explains concisely and with abundant use of diagrams and illustrations the participants, competitive site, equipment, officials, rules, penalties, and techniques and strategies for 33 competitive sports. All the major sports are included, as are such minor ones as table tennis, water polo, billiards, and auto racing. At the end of each sport's section is a one-page glossary.

410. Wright, Graeme. _Rand McNally Illustrated Dictionary of Sports_. Chicago, IL: Rand McNally, 1979. 189 p. illus. LC 78-61515.

Fifty-eight sports are grouped into 11 broad categories. Terms associated with each sport are explained with the aid of many color illustrations. Also includes important rules and brief descriptions of the sport. Other similar sources provide much more information and comprehensiveness for more sports, but this one is well formatted and better suited for the novice.

DIRECTORIES AND LOCATIONAL SOURCES

<u>COLLEGE/HIGH SCHOOL PROGRAMS AND PERSONNEL</u>

411. <u>Blue Book of College Athletics</u>. Cleveland, OH: Rohrich Corp.
      Annual. 1931-   . illus. index.

      Alphabetical list of colleges and universities providing informa-
      tion on address; names of athletic directors and coaches; team's
      color, nickname and stadium, etc. Index of colleges by states.
      (1980/81 ed. examined.)

412. <u>Blue Book of Junior College Athletics</u>. Cleveland, OH: Rohrich
      Corp. Annual. 1958-   . index. ISSN 0520-2973.

      Alphabetical listing of over 400 junior colleges providing informa-
      tion for address, names of athletic directors and coaches, team's
      color, nickname, etc. Index classifies the schools by state.
      (Based on 1980 secondary source.)

413. <u>Directory of Graduate Physical Education Programs</u>. Washington, DC:
      National Association for Sport and Physical Education, 1979.
      73 p. LC 79-106841.

      An alphabetical list of colleges and universities offering graduate
      physical education programs, with full information pertaining to
      admission, faculty and financial aid.

414. <u>Directory of Programmes, Facilities, and Faculty in Canadian Uni-
      versities</u>. Ottawa, ONT: Coaching Association of Canada, 1980.
      173 p.

      Revised and expanded version of 1974 ed. In two parts: Part A
      contains descriptions of the universities and facilities and lists
      faculty, degrees held, and the academic discipline and expertise
      for each faculty member; Part B provides subject access to the
      areas of expertise in relation to the faculty names and university
      affiliations.

415. Directory of Undergraduate Physical Education Programs. Washing-
      ton, DC: National Association for Sport and Physical Education,
      1979. 107 p. LC 79-106845.

      A companion to Directory of Graduate Physical Education Programs
      (#413), this provides similar information on about 85 undergraduate
      programs.

416. Green, Barry, and Alan Green. The Directory of Athletic Scholar-
      ships. New York: G. P. Putnam, 1981. 363 p. LC 81-4498.

      A combination of how-to guide and directory of athletic scholar-
      ships. Part I deals with the recruiting process and resume wri-
      ting. Part II consists of an alphabetical college index with names
      of sports for which scholarships are available. Part III is a list
      of colleges classified by 42 sports.

417. Information on Faculty, Facilities, and Programmes in Canadian Uni-
      versities. Rev. ed. Ottawa, ONT: Coaching Association of Cana-
      da, 1978. 358 p.

      Descriptions of coaching and training programs, facilities suitable
      for clinics and sports conferences, and faculty members interested
      in sports research are presented in alphabetical order for 23 Cana-
      dian universities.

418. NCAA Directory. Shawnee Mission, KS: National Collegiate Athletic
      Association. Annual. 1977-   . ISSN 0162-1467.

      This source covers about 860 member institutions with addresses,
      phones, and names of presidents, faculty representatives, and direc-
      tors of athletics. Arranged geographically. (Based on 1982 se-
      condary source.)

419. National Association of Intercollegiate Athletics Membership and
      District Directory. Kansas City, MO: National Association of
      Intercollegiate Athletics. Annual. 19?-   .

      Arranged geographically, by NAIA district and then by conference,
      this source lists the name, location, director, and sport sponsored
      for over 500 small and middle-sized four-year colleges. It also
      has a calendar of district championship events for each district.
      (Based on 1982 secondary source.)

420. The National Directory of College Athletics: Men's Edition. Ama-
      rillo, TX: Ray Franks Publishing. Annual. 1969-   . illus.
      index. ISSN 0547-616X.

      Organized by name of college, this lists officials employed in men's
      athletic programs at senior and junior colleges in the U. S. and
      Canada and provides information on school colors, team nicknames,
      and stadium capacities. Miscellaneous statistical information in-
      terspersed throughout. 1982-83 edition has index and some illus-
      trations. (1982-83 ed. examined.)

421. National Directory of College Athletics: Women's Edition. Ama-
      rillo, TX: Ray Franks Publishing. Annual. 1973-   . illus.
      ISSN 0092-5489.

      Annual publication of athletic officials of all senior and junior
      colleges of the U. S. and Canada. Names of colleges are arranged
      in alphabetical order, under which are listed the address, nick-
      name of team and team color, enrollment figures, the conference
      name, and officials. Other sections include tournament schedules,
      championship results, biography of the new AIAW chief, etc. (For-
      merly National Directory of Women's Athletics.) (1982-83 ed. ex-
      amined.)

422. The National Directory of High School Coaches. Montgomery, AL:
      Athletic Pub. Co. Annual. 1963-   . ISSN 0417-5956.

      Arranged alphabetically by state, then by town, and then by high
      school. Address, phone number, and coaches' names are provided for
      public and private high schools. A lengthy buyer's guide of sports
      equipment suppliers is also included. (1980/81 ed. examined.)

423. Professional Preparation Directory for Elementary School Physical
      Education. Washington, DC: National Association for Sport and
      Physical Education. Biennial. 1978-   . ISSN 0193-5747.

      A directory of 124 institutions offering specialized programs in
      elementary physical education, arranged by states. Information in-
      cludes graduate and undergraduate courses. Appendix lists univer-
      sities alphabetically. (1978 ed. examined.)

                           HALLS OF FAME

424. Jones, Thomas C. The Halls of Fame. Chicago, IL: Ferguson, 1977.
      464 p. illus. LC 77-70330.

      Lavishly illustrated with color plates and black and white photos,
      this directory describes those halls of fame which have become
      tourist attractions in the U. S. and Canada. Although the largest
      number are for specific sports, it also identifies such places as
      the Aviation Hall of Fame and the Women's Hall of Fame. Entries
      list inductees in chronological order and give a few lines of bio-
      graphical information about each.

425. Lewis, Guy, and Gerald Redmond. Sporting Heritage - A Guide to
      Halls of Fame, Special Collections and Museums in the United
      States and Canada. So. Brunswick, NJ: A. S. Barnes, 1973.
      185 p. illus. LC 73-6391.

      This directory of sport museums and halls of fame lists 50 such
      institutions in 7 geographical regions, with information on admis-
      sion dates, hours, and admission fees.

426. Soderberg, Paul, Helen Washington, and Jaques Cattell Press, eds.
      The Big Book of Halls of Fame in the United States and Canada.
      New York: Bowker, 1977. 1042 p. illus. index. LC 77-82734.

      This source identifies Halls of Fame for 30 popular pro, amateur,
      college and high school sports. It provides brief histories of
      each Hall of Fame and includes biographies for their inductees. A
      separate section lists information for the minor sports. Subject,
      year, and trivia indexes.

SPORTS ORGANIZATIONS/ASSOCIATIONS

427. International Directory of Leisure Information Resource Centres.
      Waterloo, ONT: University of Waterloo Press. Irregular.
      1980-   . ISSN 0228-2909.

      Arranged by country, this directory identifies and provides sub-
      stantial information about the collection, services, and access
      policies of 64 information and documentation centers which have as
      a major objective the collection and documentation of leisure, re-
      creation, or sport-related information. Nineteen countries are in-
      cluded. Country, subject, and center name indexes. Also known as
      Link Directory. (1980 ed. examined.)

428. Kobak, Edward T., Jr. The Comprehensive Directory of Sports Ad-
      dresses. Ludlow, VT: Kobak, 1980. 48 p. LC 80-115758.

      This directory includes addresses of major and minor leagues for
      team sports of U. S. and Canada. For certain sports such as soc-
      cer and baseball, leagues of European countries, Mexico and Japan
      are listed. There are separate sections on halls of fame and mu-
      seums; hobby organizations, dealers and periodicals; college sports
      directors, etc. Left out from this source is coverage for less
      popular team sports, such as lacrosse, cricket, polo, etc.

429. Love, Tom, ed. Who's Who in Sports: Locally, Provincially, Na-
      tionally. Waterloo, ONT: Waterloo Regional Sports Council,
      1979. 60 p.

      This source explains the structure of amateur sport in Ontario and
      Canada, listing and providing names, addresses, etc. for sports go-
      verning bodies, recreation agencies, physical education organiza-
      tions, governmental agencies, research and business organizations
      supporting amateur sports.

430. National Recreational, Sporting and Hobby Organizations of the
      United States. Washington, DC: Columbia Books. Annual.
      1981-   . ISSN 0276-5276.

      Listed are about 2,500 organizations with national memberships which
      serve recreational and avocational interests, including sports.
      Size of staff and budget, as well as meetings and publications of
      these organizations are also listed. Has subject, geographic, and
      budget indexes. (1981 ed. examined.)

431. Official AAU Code and Directory. Indianapolis, IN: Amateur Ath-
      letic Union of the U. S. Annual. 1981-   .

      The 1981 edition combines the code of the A. A. U. with four sec-
      tions of directory-type information for the A. A. U. national offi-
      cers and staff, committee divisions, administrative committees,
      other U. S. sports organizations, and the national governing bo-
      dies/sports committees for 18 amateur sports. An alphabetical in-
      dex of personal and organizational names with addresses completes
      the directory part. (Combines information with the former AAU Di-
      rectory, 19?-1980.) (1981 ed. examined.)

432. Sports Directory. Repertoire Recreation. Vanier, ONT: Sports
      Federation of Canada. Annual. 1975-   . illus.

      Identifies and provides names, addresses, and phone numbers for
      virtually all the Canadian professional, governmental, and special
      sports and recreation organizations, agencies, and clubs. Sports
      awards are listed with names of recipients. Color coded arrange-
      ment. Bilingual. (1982 ed. examined.)

                         GENERAL DIRECTORIES

433. Jeppson, Gordon D., comp. Directory of Information Resources in
      Health, Physical Education and Recreation. Washington, DC: ERIC
      Clearinghouse on Teacher Education, 1977. 33 p. (ERIC ED 137
      220).

      Covers information centers in the U. S. and Canada concerned with
      health, physical education, and recreation, and the International
      Association for Sport Information. Entries include directory-type
      information, as well as a brief description of the organization's
      purpose, information services, and costs.

434. Norback, Craig, and Peter Norback. The New American Guide to Ath-
      letics, Sports and Recreation. New York: New American Library,
      1979. 659 p. LC 79-66007.

      Although providing more information than a typical directory, this
      source's reference value is basically as a directory. Information
      on over 60 sports, listing college and university athletic programs,
      Olympic Games, sports publications, sports museums, associations,
      and careers in sports. The sports section includes the names and
      addresses of the leading clubs, leagues and stadiums; rule changes;
      and any special features, such as bicycle trails by states, ski re-
      sorts by states, and addresses of regional chapters. No index.

MISCELLANEA

435. Douglas, John A. Sports Memorabilia: A Guide to America's Fastest Growing Hobby. Des Moines, IO: Wallace-Homestead Book Co., 1976. 160 p. illus. index. LC 76-24040.

Contains descriptions and photos of many sports collectables from tickets, programs, yearbooks, etc., mostly from the author's collection. There is a glossary of terms with a single name - subject index.

436. Hoyle, Norman, et al., comps. Indexing Terms for Physical Education and Allied Fields. Albany, NY: Marathon Press, 1978. 288 p.

This compilation of more than 3,000 indexing terms seeks to provide a controlled vocabulary for physical education and its allied fields. Alphabetically arranged, terms are listed with see also (sa), broader (xx), unused (x), and preferred (see) terms. A few terms have subject subdivisions. A companion volume, Indexing Terms for Sports and Physical Education Activities, is referred to in this source's introduction. It is supposed to provide subject headings for individual and team sports and dance.

437. Pepe, Phil, and Zander Hollander. The Book of Sports Lists #3. Los Angeles, CA: Pinnacle Books, 1981. 239 p. illus.

This delightfully easy-to-browse source is the result of polling hundreds of celebrities in and out of sports. Organized by type of sport, it includes lists on sports in general ("12 Greatest Sports Songs") and for about 25 specific sports. Each list's source is credited. A veritable potpourri of sports miscellany. No index.

438. The Sports Fan's Ultimate Book of Sports Comparisons. By the Diagram Group. New York: St. Martin's Press, 1982. 192 p. illus. index. LC 81-21517.

Using copious diagrams and charts, this unique source presents comparisons between various forms of sport competitions. Some examples are team sizes for team sports; court sizes for net games;
competitive areas required for various target sports; running
speeds of winners as compared to various animals; jumping height by
pole vault, high jump or horse height jump; etc. Such information
is identified by sport type: racing sports, achievement sports
(gymnastics, skating, etc.), and opponent and tournament sports
(wrestling, fencing, golf, etc.). Subject index.

439. Standard Sports Areas for Industrial, School, Private, and Public
      Recreation Personnel. Chicago, IL: National Industrial Recrea-
      tion Association, 1973. 64 p. illus.

This manual, although compiled for the benefit of the industrial
recreation director, has reference utility since it presents in
ready-reference form the standard dimensions and specifications
for sports areas for over 36 sports commonly found in industrial
recreation programs. Hence, one finds the standards for codeball,
biddy basketball (as well as basketball), clock golf, as well as
other more common sports, but not such as skiing, golf, and sailing. Sources for these standards come from the Amateur Athletic
Union or from other official governing bodies. Table of contents
functions as an index.

440. Sugar, Bert R. The Book of Sports Quotes. New York: Quick Fox,
      1979. 149 p. illus. index. LC 78-68483.

More than 1,500 quotations uttered by and/or about sports personalities. No subject access, but has a name index.

441. Sugar, Bert R., ed. The Sports Collector's Bible. 3rd ed. In-
      dianapolis, IN: Bobbs-Merrill, 1979. 578 p. illus. index.
      LC 79-16381.

All types of sports memorabilia are listed with their market values.
Arranged by item, the section on trading cards occupies more than
half the book. Other items included are post cards, pins, auto-
graphs, guides, gum wrappers, Hartland statues, programs and
scorecards, ticket stubs, commemorative bottles and bats, sheet
music, matchbook covers, equipment, stamps, etc. Many illustrations. A collectors' registry and index to trading cards at end
of volume.

RULES SOURCES

Since there are so many published sources of rules available, this section's purpose is to identify only those that include rules for a wide variety of sports and the names and addresses of professional associations that publish rules. The first three titles are well-known reference works covering rules for a large number of sports. Most of the following organizations update their publications for rules on a regular basis, therefore correspondence with them is recommended.

442. Diagram Group. Rules of the Game. New York: Paddington Press, 1974. 320 p. illus. index. LC 73-20954.

Arranged by broad category, rules, techniques, equipment, and scoring are provided for over 400 sporting events. Well illustrated.

443. Diagram Group. The Official World Encyclopedia of Sports and Games: Rules, Techniques of Play and Equipment for Over 400 Sports and 1,000 Games. New York: Paddington Press, 1979. 543 p. illus. index. LC 79-10380.

Part 2 provides information on rules and techniques for sports.

444. Official Rules of Sports and Games. New Rochelle, NY: Sport Shelf. Biennial. 1949-   .

Incorporates official statements on specific rules for a wide variety of sports and games, as well as provides standards and measurements of playing fields, equipment specifications, scoring, etc. (1980-81 ed. examined.)

National ARCHERY Assn. of the U.S.
1750 E. Boulder St.
Colorado Springs, CO. 80909

Babe Ruth BASEBALL
P.O. Box 5000
1770 Brunswick Ave.
Trenton, NJ. 08638

Canadian Federation of Amateur
   BASEBALL
333 River Rd.
Vanier, Ontario K1L 8B9

Little League BASEBALL
P.O. Box 3485
Williamsport, PA. 17701

American BASKETBALL Assn. of the
   U.S.A.
1750 E. Boulder St.
Colorado Springs, CO. 80909

National BASKETBALL Assn.
645 Fifth Ave., 15th floor
New York, NY. 10022

National Wheelchair BASKETBALL
   Assn.
110 Seaton Bldg.
University of Kentucky
Lexington, KY. 40506

Women's Pro BASKETBALL League
604 5th Avenue
New York, NY. 10020

Canadian BOWLING Congress
147 Nantucket Blvd., Unit 1
Scarborough, Ontario M1P 2N5

Canadian Amateur BOXING Assn.
9448 68th St.
Edmonton, Alberta K1L 1T2

North American BOXING Federation
P.O. Box 12157
Capital Station
Austin, TX. 78711

Canadian CRICKET Assn.
Box 809, Adelaide St. Stn.
Toronto, Ontario M5C 2K1

U.S. CURLING Assn.
2232 Vermilion Rd.
Duluth, MN. 55803

Canadian Amateur DIVING Assn.
333 River Rd.
Ottawa, Ontario K1L 8B9

American Horse Shows Assn.
   (EQUESTRIAN)
598 Madison Ave.
New York, NY. 10022

Canadian Trotting Assn.
   (EQUESTRIAN)
233 Evans Ave.
Toronto, Ontario M8Z 1J6

National EQUESTRIAN Federation
333 River Rd.
Ottawa, Ontario K1L 8B9

U.S. Trotting Assn.
   (EQUESTRIAN)
750 Michigan Ave.
Columbus, OH. 43215

Canadian FENCING Assn.
333 River Rd.
Ottawa, Ontario K1L 8B9

U.S. FIELD HOCKEY Assn.
4415 Buffalo Rd.
N. Chili, NY. 14514

Canadian FIGURE SKATING Assn.
333 River Rd.
Ottawa, Ontario K1L 8B9

U.S. FIGURE SKATING Assn.
20 1st St.
Colorado Springs, CO. 80906

Canadian FOOTBALL League
11 King St. W., Suite 1800
Toronto, Ontario M5H 1A3

National FOOTBALL League
410 Park Ave.
New York, NY. 10022

U.S. GOLF Assn.
Golf House
Far Hills, NJ. 07931

Royal Canadian GOLF Assn.
R.R. #2
Oakville, Ontario L6J 4Z3

Canadian GYMNASTICS Federation
333 River Rd.
Ottawa, Ontario   K1L 8B9

U.S. HANDBALL Assn.
4101 Dempster St.
Skokie, IL. 60076

Amateur HOCKEY Assn.
2997 Broadmoor Valley Rd.
Colorado Springs, CO. 80906

American HOCKEY League
31 Elm St., Suite 533
Springfield, MA. 01103

Canadian Amateur HOCKEY Assn.
333 River Rd.
Vanier, Ontario K1L 8B9

National HOCKEY League
Suite 920, Sun Life Bldg.
Montreal, Quebec H3B 2W2

U.S. JUDO Federation
R.R. 21, Box 519
Terre Haute, IN. 47802

Canadian LACROSSE Assn.
333 River Rd.
Ottawa, Ontario K1L 8B9

LACROSSE Foundation
Newton White Jr. Athletic Center
Homewood, Baltimore, MD. 21218

Canadian LAWN TENNIS Assn.
333 River Rd.
Ottawa, Ontario K1L 8B9

U.S. RACQUETBALL Assn.
4101 Dempster St.
Skokie, IL. 60076

National Assn. of Amateur Oarsmen
   (ROWING)
#4 Boathouse Row
Philadelphia, PA. 19130

SHOOTING Federation of Canada
333 River Rd.
Vanier, Ontario K1L 8B9

Canadian SKI Assn.
333 River Rd.
Ottawa, Ontario K1L 8B9

Canadian SOCCER Assn.
333 River Rd.
Ottawa, Ontario K1L 8B9

North American SOCCER League
1133 Ave. of the Americas,
   Suite 3500
New York, NY. 10036

Amateur SOFTBALL Assn.
2801 N.E. 50th St.
Oklahoma City, OK. 73111

International Joint Rules Comm.
   on SOFTBALL
2801 N.E. 50th St.
Oklahoma City, OK. 73111

SOFTBALL Canada
355 River Rd., 12th floor
Vanier, Ontario K1L 8C1

Canadian SPECIAL OLYMPICS
40 St. Clair Ave., W.
Toronto, Canada M4V 1M6

SPECIAL OLYMPICS, Inc.
1701 K. St., N.W., Suite 203
Washington, DC. 20006

U.S. SQUASH Racquets Assn.
211 Ford Rd.
Bala-Cynwyd, PA. 19004

Canadian Amateur SWIMMING Assn.
333 River Rd.
Ottawa, Ontario K1L 8B9

U.S. TENNIS Assn.
51 East 42nd St.
New York, NY. 10017

Canadian TRACK & FIELD Assn.
333 River Rd.
Vanier, Ontario K1L 8B9

U.S. VOLLEYBALL Assn.
1750 E. Boulder St.
Colorado Springs, CO. 80909

Canadian WEIGHTLIFTING Federation
333 River Rd.
Vanier, Ontario K1L 8B9

U.S. WRESTLING Federation
405 W. Hall of Fame Ave.
Stillwater, OK. 74074

U.S. YACHT RACING Union
Box 209
Newport, RI. 02840

Canadian YACHTING Assn.
333 River Rd.
Vanier, Ontario K1L 8B9

The following sports organizations publish rules for more than one sport, as indicated:

Amateur Athletic Union of the U.S.
AAU House
3400 W. 86th St.
Indianapolis, IN. 46268

Boxing	Karate	Tae Kwon Do
Diving	Powerlifting	Track & Field
Judo	Swimming	Trampoline & Tumbling
Jr. Olympics		Weightlifting

National Assn. for Girls and Women in Sport
1201 16th St., N.W.
Washington, DC. 20036

Aquatics	Golf	Soccer
Archery	Gymnastics	Softball
Basketball	Ice Hockey	Swimming & Diving
Bowling	Lacrosse	Team Handball
Fencing	Racquet Sports	Tennis
Field Hockey	Skiing	Track & Field
Flag Football		Volleyball

National Collegiate Athletic Assn.
Nall Ave. at 63rd St.
P.O. Box 1906
Shawnee Mission, KS. 66201

Baseball	Lacrosse	Swimming
Basketball	Shooting (Rifle)	Track & Field
Football	Skiing	Water Polo
Ice Hockey	Soccer	Wrestling

National Federation of State High School Assns.
11724 Plaza Circle, Box 20626
Kansas City, MO. 64195

Baseball	Football	Ice Hockey
Basketball		Track & Field

National Wheelchair Athletic Assn.
2107 Templeton Gap Rd., Suite C
Colorado Springs, CO. 80907

Archery   Table Tennis   Track & Field
Swimming   Weightlifting

STATISTICAL SOURCES

445. <u>Amateur Athlete</u>. Indianapolis, IN: Amateur Athletic Union of the
      United States. Annual. 19?-1978. illus. ISSN 0002-6808.

      A complete annual record of national and world championships for
      the year under coverage. There is a separate section for the
      Junior Olympic Games. Lots of action photos. (1978 ed. examined.)

446. Bukata, Jim. <u>ABC's Wide World of Sports Record Book</u>. Rev. ed.
      New York: Stadia Sports Pub., 1974. 222 p. illus. LC 73-
      84461.

      This statistical chronology is a compilation of facts, figures, and
      dates of sports which have been covered on ABC's Wide World of
      Sports television series.

447. Clark, Patrick. <u>Sports Firsts</u>. New York: Facts on File, 1981.
      262 p. illus. bibl. index. LC 80-26795.

      This source chronicles the first time events of sports, beginning
      with the more popular ones like baseball, football, basketball,
      etc., to the exotic flying sports. Apart from the first game of
      each sport, events covered range from the trivial (first paid ad-
      mission) to the interesting (first umpire fired for dishonesty),
      to the important facts (first triple crown winner). A detailed
      table of contents serves as a subject index. There is an index of
      sport personalities.

448. <u>The Corpus Almanac's Canadian Sports Annual</u>. Ed. by M. J. Fawcett.
      Toronto, ONT: Corpus Publishers. Annual. 1977-   . illus.
      ISSN 0704-7274.

      Much more than just a source for records, this first edition is in-
      valuable for identifying and explaining how sports are organized in
      Canada at the national, provincial and local level. Included are
      brief articles providing the history and activities of professional,
      amateur and educational sports associations for about 80 different
      sports. Within each sport section are listed the names of 16 cham-
      pions for the prior year's season. A directory of sports associa-
      tions completes the volume. (1977 ed. examined.)

449. Hollander, Zander, and David Schulz. The Illustrated Sports Re-
         cord Book. New York: New American Library, 1975. 240 p. illus.

450. McWhirter, Norris, et al. Guinness Book of Sports Records, Winners
         and Champions. Rev. ed. New York: Sterling, 1982. 352 p.
         illus. index. LC 81-85045.

      This is a paperback edition of the 1980 Sterling publication. An
      expanded revision of the Guinness Sports Record Book, this is a
      comprehensive record of winners and champions for a total of 71 ma-
      jor and minor sports. Alphabetical by sport, each section begins
      with a short history, followed by record categories, such as the
      longest game, fastest, slowest, youngest, etc. Also includes re-
      cords for games and pastimes such as chess, darts, frisbee. Re-
      sults of 1980 Olympic Games are listed in this edition. An ex-
      cellent index by sport with subject subdivisions.

451. National Collegiate Championships. Shawnee Mission, KS: National
         Collegiate Athletic Association. Annual. 1954-   . ISSN 0077-
         3824.

      For all the sports included in the National Collegiate Championship
      series are listed the yearly records for the athletes of each col-
      lege. (Formerly, National Collegiate Championships Record Book,
      ISSN 0148-9798.) (Based on 1982 secondary source.)

452. Neft, David S., et al. Grosset and Dunlap's All-Sports World Re-
         cord Book. New York: Grosset and Dunlap, 1976. 320 p. LC 74-
         18879.

      "Presents in-depth records, champions, standings, plus annual and
      career leaders for thirty-two major sports." Not all sports get
      "in-depth" treatment; most have the winners' names and year, with-
      out the actual winning records.

453. The Official Associated Press Sports Almanac. New York: Dell Pub.
         Annual. 1974-   . illus. ISSN 0094-3274.

      Arranged by sport, a brief history of nearly 100 sports is fol-
      lowed by records for the year and often records for previous years.
      Yearly schedules for many sports also provided. (1979 ed. exa-
      mined.)

454. Smith, Norman Lewis, ed. Sports and Games Almanac. New York:
         Facts on File, 1979. 442 p. illus. LC 79-484.

      An alphabetical sport-by-sport arrangement with records and rank-
      ings of 1978's competitions and tournaments. Brief descriptions
      are given for each sport, with highlights of major events for some.
      Inclusion of unusual sports, such as frog jumping, kite flying,
      makes this more comprehensive than a regular almanac. No index,
      but table of contents provides cross references. An obituary sec-
      tion is included.

31.
SPORTS AND PHYSICAL
EDUCATION: TOPICAL

HISTORY OF SPORT

BIBLIOGRAPHICAL SOURCES

455. Barney, Robert Knight, ed. A Source Bibliography - The History of
      Sport and Physical Education. London, ONT: University of West-
      ern Ontario, D. B. Weldon Library, 1979. 57 p.

      Unannotated list of more than 1,000 books from the Weldon Library
      published between 1889 and 1979. Arranged alphabetically by au-
      thor. Sources included describe and analyze play, sport, games,
      dance, exercise and leisure activities of people of all civiliza-
      tions throughout history and prehistory. Update edition planned
      every three years.

456. Dickinson, John Stewart. Annotated Bibliography of Historical Wri-
      tings Related to Physical Education in National Professional Phy-
      sical Education Journals and Proceedings in North America During
      the Last Decade (January 1963 - December 1972). Eugene, OR:
      University of Oregon, School of Health, Physical Education, and
      Recreation. Microform Publications, 1974. 62 p. index.

      This bibliography, in microfiche format, is the author's masters
      thesis completed in 1973 at the University of Oregon. It contains
      over 200 annotated references to articles and proceedings from 8
      scholarly journals pertaining to historical writings on physical
      education. Arranged in chronological order. Subject index.

457. Gee, Ernest R. Early American Sporting Books, 1734 to 1844 -- A
      Few Brief Notes. 1928; reprint. New York: Haskell House, 1971.
      61 p. illus. LC 75-167737.

      This reprint of the 1928 work identifies and provides much histori-
      cal background for 22 sporting books and magazines published in
      America between 1734 and 1844.

458. Henderson, Robert W., comp. Early American Sport. 3rd rev. and
      enlarged ed. Rutherford, NJ: Fairleigh Dickinson University
      Press, 1977. 309 p. illus. index. LC 74-30537.

This expanded and revised bibliography of the 1937 and 1953 checklists covers books by American and foreign authors published in America prior to 1860. Arranged by author, the subject index provides access by sports with chronological title entries.

459. Mutimer, Brian T. P., comp. Canadian Graduating Essays, Theses and Dissertations Relating to the History and Philosophy of Sport, Physical Education and Recreation. Rev. ed. Ottawa, ONT: Canadian Association for Health, Physical Education, and Recreation, 1980. 35 p. bibl.

Theses and dissertations on sports, physical education, and recreation are organized into history, philosophy and biography sections.

460. Sawula, Lorne, and A. Metcalfe. Bibliography: History of Sport and Physical Education in Canada. Windsor, ONT: University of Windsor, 1970. 44 p.

Primary and secondary sources of published and unpublished materials are listed alphabetically by author within categories for the history of Canadian sports and physical education in general, and football, hockey, lacrosse, basketball, winter sports, summer sports, and some outdoor recreational activities.

461. Sawula, Lorne. Repository of Primary and Secondary Sources for Canadian History of Sport and Physical Education. Halifax, Nova Scotia: Dalhousie University, School of Physical Education, 1974. 170 p. index.

A listing of the primary and some secondary source material (theses, archives, manuscripts, films, etc.) of interest to sport historians found in over 40 Canadian libraries and research centers. Author and subject index.

462. Zeigler, Earle F., M. L. Howell, and M. Trekell, eds. Research in the History, Philosophy, and International Aspects of Physical Education and Sport: Bibliographies and Techniques. Champaign, IL: Stripes Pub., 1971. 350 p. LC 76-26892.

Bibliographic essays and lengthy bibliographies devoted to research and the development of knowledge about the historical, philosophical, comparative and international aspects of physical education and sports. Citations cover period up through 1967.

OTHER

463. Brown, Gene, ed. New York Times Encyclopedia of Sports. 15 vols. New York: Arno Press, 1979-80. illus. bibl. index. LC 79-19980.

This set brings together articles and photos from the N. Y. Times, providing an historical documentary of the sport and its players. Each volume has appendix containing records, selected readings and a name index. Titles of individual volumes are: v. 1 Football. 198 p. LC 79-19951; v. 2 Baseball. 213 p. LC 79-19930; v. 3 Basketball. 214 p. LC 79-19939; v. 4 Track & Field. 214 p. LC 79-20181; v. 5 Golf. 206 p. LC 79-20195; v. 6 Tennis. 210 p. LC 79-19940; v. 7 Boxing. 205 p. LC 79-19945; v. 8 Soccer and Professional Hockey. 222 p. LC 79-20372; v. 9 Winter Sports. 194 p. LC 79-19932; v. 10 Outdoor Sports. 222 p. LC 79-19949; v. 11 Indoor Sports. 202 p. LC 79-19944; v. 12 Water Sports. 205 p. LC 79-20179; v. 13 Horse Racing and Auto Racing. 211 p. LC 79-19938; v. 14 Index and Bibliography. 83 p.; v. 15 Update 1980. 312 p.

464. Fetros, John G. This Day in Sports: A Diary of Major Sports Events. Novato, CA: Newton K. Gregg, 1974. 264 p. LC 74-75882.

This source is arranged in diary format for the 365 days of the year. Major events in sports, tracing back to the early 1700's, are identified chronologically, with as many as 35 or more happenings on some dates. Without an index, this is only useful for finding out what took place on certain days; or if the date is known, to determine in which year the event took place.

465. Findling, John E., and Angela Lumpkin, comps. Directory of Scholars Identifying with the History of Sport. 2nd ed. n.p.: North American Society for Sport History, 1979. 86 p. index.

Sponsored by NASSH, information for this directory is obtained from questionnaires. The 277 respondents are arranged alphabetically with address, phone, areas of research interest, publications, specific projects, courses taught, and membership in sport-related organizations. Separate topical index, and geographic index.

466. Gipe, George. The Great American Sports Book. New York: Doubleday, 1978. 570 p. illus. index. LC 77-4707.

Arranged by 11 sections, this unique source chronicles the feats, records, personalities, activities, and historical accounts of sports in the U. S. from the end of the Civil War. Contained in each section (which covers 10 years) is one chapter that describes the sports events that made news during a single year of that decade. Also, each section contains brief rundowns for every year in the decade, listing results of major athletic competitions as well as other sports happenings that happen to be "significant, funny, tragic, or outrageous." Many black and white reproductions of photos.

467. Hart, Harold H. Physical Feats That Made History. New York: Hart Pub., 1974. 388 p. illus. index. LC 73-82003.

Arranged chronologically from 900 B. C. to 1973, important physical feats, most of which are sports feats, are described in brief sketches. Name/subject index allows access by sports.

OLYMPIC GAMES

The quadrennial events of the Olympics generate a surge of publications before the Games take place. Such sources typically provide a complete record from the beginning up through the latest Olympics, with information also provided for the upcoming one. Such a pattern of publication makes it unnecessary to include reference materials for each of the Games. For this section coverage has, therefore, been restricted to the last two, i.e., 1976 and 1980. A search for similar sources that would include results of the 1980 Summer Olympics has been unsuccessful. No doubt, such publications will surface shortly before the next Summer Olympics to be held in Los Angeles, California. In the meantime, one can locate the results of the 1980 Games in such general statistical sources as Guinness Book of Sports Records, Winners and Champions (#450) and The World Almanac and Book of Facts, 1981 or 1982 editions.

BIOGRAPHICAL SOURCES

468. Cosentino, Frank, and Glynn Leyshon. Olympic Gold - Canada's Winners in the Summer Games. Toronto, ONT: Holt, Rinehart and Winston of Canada, 1975. 147 p. illus. bibl. LC 75-18456.

This is an "official history of Canadian Summer Olympic Gold Medal winners as authorized by the Organizing Committee of the 1976 Olympic Games." Beginning with the first medal won in 1904, this source describes the struggles, incredible determination, and self-sacrifice of gold medalists in chronological order of the Olympic Games up to 1972. A table lists names of gold, silver and bronze medal winners and the Olympic events for which they won the medals.

469. Libby, Bill. Stars of the Olympics. New York: Hawthorn Books, 1975. 189 p. illus. index. LC 73-21313.

Biographical information on winners is gathered from interviews, and grouped into the years of the events. A name index provides the cross references.

ENCYCLOPEDIAS

470.   Baker, Eugene H., ed. XIII Olympic Winter Games. Lake Placid.
        1980. Chicago, IL: Rand McNally, 1979. 230 p. illus. index.
        LC 79-89008.

        To those sport fans of the winter games, this colorfully illustrat-
        ed source serves as an encyclopedia to the history and records of
        all the winter games up through 1976. Different chapters cover
        eight events, with the games chronologically arranged. Evaluation
        of the top contenders for the 1980 games and their portraits round
        up each chapter. A few introductory pages explain the governance
        structure of the U. S. Olympic Committee, which is responsible for
        this publication. Name index.

471.   Brennan, Gale. The XXII Summer Olympic Games - Moscow 1980. Mil-
        waukee, WI: Ideals Pub. Co., 1979. 80 p. illus. LC 80-110264.

        Published just before the 1980 Moscow Olympics, this source serves
        as a reference to the rules, past winners up through 1976 and their
        records, and a schedule of the summer games. Each event is covered
        in 2 - 3 pages of text with color photos. The names of potential
        winners in 1980 are given for some.

472.   de Groote, Roger. Sports Olympiques Album Officiel - Montreal 1976.
        (Olympic Sports Official Album - Montreal 1976.) Toronto, ONT:
        Little, Brown and Co., 1975. 311 p. illus. bibl. LC 75-29984.

        This official album of the Montreal Olympics is a colorful encyclo-
        pedia which documents the events and past records. It explains in
        French and English the meanings of the flag, motto, flame, opening
        and closing ceremony, etc. before dealing with individual events.
        A brief descriptive history of origin, rules, and other interesting
        anecdotes (such as the invention by Dunlop of inflatable bicycle
        tires and valve), accompany the complete records up through 1972.
        The last section traces the Olympic movements in the U. S. and the
        roles of the U. S. Olympic Committee.

473.   Kamper, Erich. Encyclopedia of the Olympic Games. 1st ed. New
        York: McGraw-Hill, 1972. 360 p. bibl. LC 71-38508.

        This source, in English, French, and German, covers the Olympic
        winners from 1896 to 1968. Events are grouped by type in a table
        of contents which serves as an index. A better source is Killanin's
        The Olympic Games 1980 (#474).

474.   Killanin, Michael Morris, and John Rodda, eds. The Olympic Games
        1980. New York: Macmillan, 1980. 319 p. illus. index. LC
        79-13768.

        An encyclopedia and record book of the games from the first Olympic
        Games through 1976. Extensive descriptions of both summer and win-
        ter games, and history of the International Olympic Committee. In-
        cludes brief biographies of winners. A table of contents and index
        of persons provide the necessary access points. This publication
        precedes the 1980 Moscow Games and revises the 1976 edition.

STATISTICAL SOURCES

475. Guinness Book of Olympic Records. Ed. by Norris D. McWhirter, et
        al. New York: Bantam Books. Quadrennial. 1964-   . illus.

      This source covers every past Olympics, and in the latest edition
      provides a "complete roll of Olympic medal winners (1896-1976, in-
      cluding 1906) for the 28 sports (7 winter and 21 summer) to be con-
      tested in the 1980 celebrations..." Other useful information is
      included to aid the spectators in better understanding the games.
      (1979 ed. examined.)

476. The Olympic Guide. By John V. Grombach. New York: Times Books.
        Quadrennial. 1960-   . illus. ISSN 0198-716X.

      Grombach has been the editor of this official Olympic guide since
      the 1960 games. Apart from the records of each event, a unique
      feature is the tables of championships by nation. A schedule of the
      upcoming games is included. (1980 ed. examined.)

477. United States Olympic Book. Colorado Springs, CO: United States
        Olympic Committee. Quadrennial. 1928?-   . illus.

      Report of Olympic records by the U. S. Olympic Committee. Issues
      on 1928-1964 include reports of the 2nd - 9th Olympic Winter Games;
      1952-1964 includes reports of the 1st - 4th Pan American Games 1951-
      1963. (Based on 1982 secondary source.)

                              OTHER

478. Benagh, Jim. Incredible Olympic Feats. New York: McGraw-Hill,
        1976. 178 p. illus. LC 75-33237.

      Different from other books on Olympic Games history, this source
      provides references to the greatest upsets and the "incredibles"
      of all Olympic events from 1896 to 1972. With 2 - 3 page descrip-
      tions each, it tells the behind-the-scene happenings that make the
      particular achievements such "incredible feats." Feats included
      are medals won at age 73, boy wonder of all time, 10 soccer goals
      scored in a game, record number of medals won, triple loop jump in
      figure skating, etc. Last 30 pages list winners and records by
      events and years.

479. Carroll, Walter J., ed. Olympics Film Finder. 1981 Business ed.
        New York: Olympic Media Information, 1981. 51 p.

      Audio-visual programs listed by title and subject. (Based on 1980
      secondary source.)

480. Danaher, Mary A. The Commemorative Coinage of Modern Sports. So.
        Brunswick, NJ: A. S. Barnes, 1978. 183 p. illus. bibl. index.
        LC 75-20610.

First half of this book introduces Olympic Games coins, with the
remainder devoted to coins of regional games, such as Commonwealth
games, Pan-American games, World Cup Soccer, etc. Most of the
coins are illustrated with photos of coins from the author's personal collection. Other information includes mintage, mint marks,
size, and metallic content. Subject index.

HANDICAPPED AND SPORTS/PHYSICAL EDUCATION

BIBLIOGRAPHICAL SOURCES

481. Annotated Listing of Films: Physical Education and Recreation for
      Impaired, Disabled, and Handicapped Persons. 2nd ed. Washing-
      ton, DC: Information and Research Utilization Center, American
      Alliance for Health, Physical Education and Recreation, 1976.
      119 p. index. (ERIC ED 150 828).

      Organized alphabetically by title, this source lists films and the
      names and addresses of the distributors, as well as provides lengthy
      summaries of the film contents. Subject index at the back allows
      access by handicapping condition and physical activity.

482. Annotated Research Bibliography in Physical Education, Recreation,
      and Psychomotor Function of Mentally Retarded Persons. Washing-
      ton, DC: Information and Research Utilization Center, American
      Alliance for Health, Physical Education and Recreation, 1975.
      285 p. (ERIC ED 113 907).

      A comprehensive bibliography (mostly annotated) of research studies
      for this special population reported in periodical literature, the-
      ses and dissertations, and conference proceedings for the time per-
      iod 1889-1975. Five subject indexes focusing on characteristics of
      subjects, particular physical education, recreation, and psycho-
      motor activities and tests and evaluative instruments precede and
      provide access to the two sections of entries alphabetically ar-
      ranged by author.

483. Aubert, Halldis. Handicap - Sport: A Preliminary Bibliography on
      Sport for the Disabled and the Ill, 1960-1973. 2nd ed. n.p.
      1973. 186 p. (ERIC ED 080 532).

      International coverage of approximately 2,000 books, periodicals,
      theses, dissertations, research projects, etc. Listed alphabeti-
      cally by author in the main section. Index allows access by ac-
      tivities and handicapping conditions.

484. A Bibliography of Surveys in Physical Education and Recreation Pro-
      grams for Impaired, Disabled, and Handicapped Persons. Washing-
      ton, DC: American Alliance for Health, Physical Education and
      Recreation, 1973. 13 p. (ERIC ED 092 557).

      Arranged alphabetically by author into two sections, "General Sur-
      veys" and "Professional Preparation Surveys," this 114 item bib-
      liography lists national, regional, state and local surveys of pro-
      grams for adapted physical education, community/municipal/thera-
      peutic recreation, sport and athletic programs for participants
      with handicapping conditions. Topic and state indexes in front.
      Some of the sources listed can be found in professional journals,
      but majority are theses and state/local publications.

485. Buell, Charles. Bibliography on Physical Education. Philadelphia,
      PA: Association for Education of the Visually Handicapped, 1974.
      8 p. (ERIC ED 100 092).

      Annotated listing of 75 books, articles, periodicals, newsletters,
      and A/V materials for use in physical education programming.

486. Competitive Athletic Programs for Impaired, Disabled, and Handi-
      capped Persons: Information Sheet. Rev. ed. Washington, DC:
      Information and Research Utilization Center, American Alliance
      for Health, Physical Education and Recreation, 1977. 21 p.

      Lists by handicapping condition the associations concerned with
      sports and provides a subject index by sport and condition to
      print materials and films listed in the "Bibliography" section.
      Entries for films are annotated.

487. Geddes, Dolores M., comp. Integrating Persons with Handicapping
      Conditions Into Regular Physical Education Programs. Rev. ed.
      by Liane Summerfield. Washington, DC: Information and Research
      Utilization Center, American Alliance for Health, Physical Educa-
      tion and Recreation, 1977. 79 p. index. (ERIC ED 159 856).

      Beginning with brief articles on mainstreaming and a clarification
      of terms, this source is composed of a lengthy annotated bibliogra-
      phy organized in 3 parts. Entries within the parts are arranged
      alphabetically by author or title. Books, journal articles and
      audio-visual materials are included. Preceding the main biblio-
      graphy section is an index organized by handicapping conditions
      and subject areas.

488. Geddes, Dolores M., comp. Physical Education and Recreation for
      Individuals with Multiple Handicapping Conditions: References
      and Resources. Rev. ed. by Liane Summerfield. Washington, DC:
      Information and Research Utilization Center, American Alliance
      for Health, Physical Education and Recreation, 1978. 40 p.
      (ERIC ED 159 855).

Organized in 3 parts, this source identifies documents (journal
articles, books, and ERIC documents), audio-visual aids, and organizations focusing on physical education and recreation for individuals with multiple handicapping conditions. Part 1 is grouped by
multiple handicapping condition and lists and abstracts documents.
Part 2 lists alphabetically by title and abstracts audio-visual
aids. Part 3 list organizations with their addresses, as well as
provides names and addresses of relevant periodicals.

489. Gilbertson, Kristina. Physical Education, Recreation and Sports for
     Individuals with Hearing Impairments. Washington, DC: Informa-
     tion and Research Utilization Center, American Alliance for
     Health, Physical Education and Recreation, 1976. 122 p. (ERIC
     ED 146 716).

     Organized by activity are annotated references to books and journal
     articles on physical education, recreation, art, dance, drama, mu-
     sic, and swimming for individuals with learning impairment. Audio-
     visual materials are listed with summaries in a separate section
     at the end. Also included are reprints of 8 articles and a direc-
     tory of national organizations for the deaf.

490. Graue, Nancy. Challenging Opportunities for Special Populations
     in Aquatic, Outdoor, and Winter Activities. Washington, DC: In-
     formation and Research Utilization Center, American Alliance for
     Health, Physical Education and Recreation, 1974. 79 p. index.
     (ERIC ED 150 827).

     Organized into 3 broad sections -- aquatics, winter activities, and
     outdoor activities -- printed materials, audio-visual materials,
     assisted devices and adapted equipment are identified and annotated.
     Indexes at the beginning of each section provide access by handi-
     capping condition, activities, and teaching methods. Names and ad-
     dresses of resource contacts and reprints of 12 articles complete
     this source.

491. Graue, Nancy. Physical Education and Recreation for Cerebral Pal-
     sied Individuals. Washington, DC: Information and Research
     Utilization Center, American Alliance for Health, Physical Educa-
     tion and Recreation, 1976. 124 p.

     Following an article which discusses the nature and causes of cere-
     bral palsy, are annotated listings of general references; a section
     on motor performance; activity resources (physical education, aqua-
     tics, recreation, music, art, and dance); and a section on addi-
     tional resources (adapted equipment, audio-visual materials, etc.).
     Reprints of 10 articles complete this source.

492. Information Sheet on Aquatics for the Impaired, Disabled, and Han-
     dicapped. Developed by the Council for National Cooperation in
     Aquatics and the AAHPER. Washington, DC: Information and Re-
     search Utilization Center, American Alliance for Health, Physical
     Education and Recreation, 1972. 28 p. (ERIC ED 080 515).

An annotated bibliography of books, periodical articles, and dissertations arranged in alphabetical order by author. A brief subject index in the front identifies the entries by handicap and specific subject. A resources section lists people and agencies interested and involved in aquatics for the handicapped.

493. Information Update. Washington, DC: Information and Research
    Utilization Center, American Alliance for Health, Physical Education and Recreation. Monthly. 1977-May 1979. index.

    This very useful monthly bibliography ceased in May 1979. Organized by type of publication, it lists and provides brief summaries of books, journal articles, published and unpublished papers, research reports, and instructional aids about physical education, recreation, and sports focusing on handicapped individuals. Two indexes are provided: 1) a subject index composed of 8 smaller indexes for handicapping conditions, type of physical education activity or sport, facilities, etc.; and 2) an index of organizations.

494. McCally, Michael, comp. Bibliography: Therapeutic Horsemanship.
    Wilsonville, OR: North American Riding for the Handicapped Association, 1978. 23 p.

    A comprehensive bibliography of 139 titles of published and unpublished materials, including audiovisuals, on riding for the handicapped.

495. Physical Education and Leisure Time: A Selective Bibliography.
    Exceptional Child Bibliography Series, No. 612. Reston, VA:
    Council for Exceptional Children, 1973. 23 p. index. (ERIC
    ED 090 705).

    This annotated bibliography contains about 95 references and abstracts on physical education and leisure time activities for handicapped children. These references were selected from the Council's Information Center's computer file and represent a variety of sources published between 1962 and 1973. Author and subject indexes. Subject index provides access by type of handicap and physical education activity.

496. Physical Education and Recreation. Exceptional Child Bibliography
    Series. Arlington, VA: Council for Exceptional Children, 1971.
    19 p. index. (ERIC ED 051 593).

    One in a series of over 50 similar selected listings relating to handicapped and gifted, this bibliography contains 73 references and abstracts on physical education and recreation selected from Exceptional Child Education Abstracts. References include research reports, conference papers, journal articles, texts, and program guides. Author and subject indexes.

497. Physically Handicapped: Adaptive Devices. Columbus, OH: National
    Center on Educational Media and Materials for the Handicapped,
    1977. 22 p. index. (ERIC ED 145 663).

Selected from the National Instructional Materials Information System, this bibliography lists and describes 76 adaptive devices and equipment items for working with physically handicapped students, with particular emphasis on physical education, recreation, and other daily living skills. Publisher, title, and subject indexes.

498. Recreation for the Handicapped: A Selection of Recent Books and Pamphlets. Chicago, IL: National Easter Seal Society for Crippled Children and Adults, 1975. 12 p. (ERIC ED 113 905).

Listing of 96 books and pamphlets for adapted physical education, recreational activities, and camping.

499. Summerfield, Liane. Physical Education, Recreation, and Related Programs for Autistic and Emotionally Disturbed Children. Washington, DC: Information and Research Utilization Center, American Alliance for Health, Physical Education and Recreation, 1976. 124 p. (ERIC ED 149 535).

This source combines practical information about the characteristics and physical education needs of autistic and emotionally disturbed children with annotated bibliographies on physical education, perceptual-motor experiences, recreation and play experiences, and art, dance and music activities for these two populations. Also included are descriptions of on-going programs in physical education and recreation for these 2 groups, explanations of specific activities, and article reprints.

DIRECTORIES AND LOCATIONAL SOURCES

500. Library of Congress. Division for the Blind and Physically Handicapped. Sports: A Selected List of Books That Have Appeared in Talking Book Topics and Braille Book Review. Washington, DC: Library of Congress, 1977. 56 p. (plus record). LC 77-13139. (SUDOC LC 19.11:Sp6).

A listing of talking books and books in braille on various sports and sports topics.

501. Library of Congress. National Library Service for the Blind and Physically Handicapped. Sports and Games for Handicapped Persons. Washington, DC: Government Printing Office, 1979. 21 p. (SUDOC LC 19.4/2:79-1).

Organizations and a brief description of their purpose are listed in three sections: sports, games and information centers. A final section lists titles and addresses of periodicals devoted to sports and recreation for the handicapped.

502. Sherrill, C., and G. Tymeson, eds. Directory of Resources in Phy-
      sical Education and Recreation for the Handicapped: A Project
      of the National Consortium on Physical Education and Recreation
      for the Handicapped. Denton, TX: College of Education, Texas
      Women's Univ., 1979. 366 p. (ERIC ED 179 049).

      Lists and provides information for about 150 professionals in the
      field of physical education and recreation for the handicapped.

503. Summerfield, Liane, ed. Guide to Information Systems in Physical
      Education and Recreation for Impaired, Disabled, and Handicapped
      Persons. Washington, DC: Information and Research Utilization
      Center, American Alliance for Health, Physical Education and Re-
      creation, 1975. 41 p. (ERIC ED 115 616).

      Information centers listed in this guide are organized into 5 sec-
      tions according to their concentration. Each entry provides name,
      address, a description of the center and its services.

OTHER POPULATIONS: WOMEN, BLACKS, AND AGED

WOMEN - BIBLIOGRAPHICAL SOURCES

504. Eide, Margaret. Women and Sports. Bibliography Series #38.
Ypsilanti, MI: Eastern Michigan University, 1978. 41 p. (ERIC
ED 156 631).

Articles listed cover women in professional sports, amateur athletics, intramurals, physiological and psychological aspects of women athletes, and equality for women in sport.

505. Remley, Mary L. Women in Sport - A Guide to Information Sources.
Sports, Games, and Pastimes Information Guide Series, vol. 10.
Detroit, MI: Gale, 1980. 139 p. index. LC 80-14773.

This guide covers reference works, biographies, technique books,
periodicals and films of major sports for women. Organized into
4 parts, entries are annotated but not numbered, with author, title,
and subject indexes.

506. Spirduso, Waneen Wyrick, ed. Bibliography of Research Involving
Female Subjects. Washington, DC: American Alliance for Health,
Physical Education and Recreation, 1974. 212 p. LC 75-313612.

This bibliography results from a survey sent to 200 colleges and
universities requesting citations of theses and dissertations written by women or on women. Entries are by author and are grouped
into 9 subject areas from motor learning, psychology, physiology,
etc. to recreation. A list of participating colleges is given.

507. Women in Sports - Spring 1977 - Sports Kit. Washington, DC: Women's Equity Action League, 1978. 76 p. (ERIC ED 179 492).

A guide to information about Women's Equity Action League, its in-
ternship program, excerpts from Title IX sections on sport, memo-
randum regarding legal obligations of school officials, etc. Bibliographies include one for children's books, an extensive general
bibliography, and for audio-visual materials.

DIRECTORIES AND LOCATIONAL SOURCES

508. AIAW Directory. Washington, DC: Association for Intercollegiate
     Athletics for Women, American Alliance for Health, Physical Edu-
     cation and Recreation. Annual. 1976/77-   . ISSN 0362-6636.

     This source supersedes in part the AIAW Handbook - Directory, 1971-
     1976. It lists athletic programs for women at 2 and 4 year col-
     leges which are members of AIAW, and provides information on scho-
     larships available to female athletes. Institution list is ar-
     ranged alphabetically by college and program/aid list is alpha-
     betical by sport and state. (Based on 1980 secondary source.)

509. Stanek, Carolyn. The Complete Guide to Women's College Athletics.
     Chicago, IL: Contemporary Books, 1981. 244 p. bibl. index.
     LC 80-70635.

     About one half of this source is non-reference in nature, since it
     is practical information about Title IX, recruiting, college visits,
     etc. The reference information is located in the 2 lengthy appen-
     dixes: one a listing of colleges and the types of scholarships
     they offer; and the other a listing of women's sports foundations'
     sports camps.

STATISTICAL AND BIOGRAPHICAL SOURCES

510. McDonald, David, and Lauren Drewery. For the Record - Canada's
     Greatest Women Athletes. Rexdale, ONT: Mesa Associates, 1981.
     270 p. illus. bibl.

     Biographies of 37 greatest women athletes from alpine skiing to
     wheelchair sports. The 3 pages of information for each includes
     her career highlights and a portrait. Also includes a record of
     Canada's women Olympic medal winners, Canada's Sports Hall of Fame
     and winners of other trophies. Short bibliography but no index,
     although the table of contents indicates one.

511. McWhirter, Norris, et al. Guinness Book of Women's Sports Records.
     New York: Sterling Pub., 1979. 192 p. illus. index. LC 78-
     66315.

     Similar in style and content to the Guinness Sports Record Book
     (#450), this source provides the names of women title holders and
     their records from their first recorded entry into the sport up
     through 1978. Over 46 sports are included.

512. U. S. Commission on Civil Rights. More Hurdles to Clear - Women
     and Girls in Competitive Athletics. Clearinghouse Publication
     No. 63. Washington, DC: United States Commission on Civil
     Rights, 1980. 87 p. illus. bibl. LC 80-602854. (SUDOC
     CR1.10:63).

A useful statistical source of comparative data for male and female participation in sports. Includes several tabulated charts
and graphs. Appendixes set forth HEW's jurisdiction under Title
IX, and a copy of the text of the Federal Register's "Nondiscrimi-
nation on the Basis of Sex."

BLACKS AND AGED

513. Davis, Lenwood G., and Belinda S. Daniels, comps. Black Athletes
      in the United States: A Bibliography of Books, Articles, Auto-
      biographies, and Biographies on Black Professional Athletes in
      the U. S. 1800-1981. Westport, CT: Greenwood, 1981. 265 p.
      index. LC 81-6334.

Beginning with a 3-page coverage of major reference books on baseball, basketball, boxing, football, golf and tennis, one-third of
the volume contains some 700 annotated titles of books by and about
black athletes. The remaining two-thirds includes over 3,000 articles on the same 6 sports. Listings of boxing champions, Hall
of Fame members, most valuable players, black athletes in films,
etc. are found in the appendixes. Name index only.

514. Lyon, Lesley. A National Directory of Physical Fitness Programs
      for Older Adults. Saranac Lake, NY: North Country Community
      College Press, 1981. 157 p. LC 81-80242.

Designed to help the healthy and limited-movement-capacity elderly
locate colleges and universities in the U. S. that offer physical
fitness programs for older adults. Programs' scope explained in
entries.

515. Terauds, Juris, comp. Physical Activity for the Elderly. Del Mar,
      CA: Academic Publishers, 1979. 140 p.

This bibliography includes articles on the biomechanical and physiological aspects of physical activity for the elderly. All entries,
arranged by author, are listed in the first section. Lengthy annotations are provided in the second section for some of the citations listed in the first half.

MEDICAL, PHYSIOLOGICAL, AND PHYSICAL FITNESS ASPECTS

BIBLIOGRAPHICAL SOURCES

516. Arora, Ved P. Physical Fitness - A Bibliography. Regina, SASK: Provincial Library, Bibliographic Services Division, 1973. 31 p. index.

A catalog of references (some annotated) for over 200 books, published between 1939-1971 which are located in Saskatchewan libraries on basic exercises and training. Main section is arranged by author with a title index.

517. Ferris, Blake F., and Maureen Artichuk. Fitness Canada/CPHA Labour Fitness and Lifestyle Project - Program Director Resource Materials. n.p., 1981. 40 p. (SIRC GV 481 #11710).

Articles, books and media on fitness and lifestyle available from SIRC, Fitness Canada, and Health and Welfare Canada, published after 1970. A separate section for French titles. Includes list of government fitness consultants, Canadian universities and community colleges. Only media and newsletter titles are annotated.

518. Hay, James G. A Bibliography of Biomechanics Literature. 4th ed. Iowa City, IO: University of Iowa, 1981. 425 p. LC 81-86371.

This computer typeset edition is a big improvement over the previous one which was manually produced. The coverage is expanded to include books, articles and dissertations up to 1980. In alphabetical sequence by authors, all citations are grouped into 20 subject sections. The one on sports has subdivisions into individual sports. Subjects range from basic movements to teaching of biomechanics. Includes foreign publications.

519. Hughston, Jack Chandler, and Kenneth S. Clarke, eds. Bibliography of Sports Medicine. Chicago, IL: American Academy of Orthopaedic Surgeons, 1970. 96 p.

An introduction to the interdisciplinary literature with a cross index. (Based on 1977 secondary source.)

520. Library of Congress. Science and Technology Division. Science
      Tracer Bullet TB 79-5; Sports Medicine Bibliography. Washington,
      DC: Government Printing Office, 1979. 9 p. (SUDOC LC 33.10
      79-5).

      Bibliography of books and some NTIS reports in the Science and Tech-
      nology Division of the Library of Congress. Standard bibliographi-
      cal information provided, plus call numbers. No annotations.

521. National Diabetes Information Clearinghouse. Sports and Exercise
      for People with Diabetes - Selected Annotations. Washington,
      DC: U. S. Department of Health and Human Services, 1981. 19 p.
      index. (SUDOC HE 20.3316:Sp6).

      Organized by the categories of public and patient resources and
      professional resources are listings and annotations for print and
      non-print materials covering the role of sports and exercise in
      the lives of people with diabetes. Within each category the en-
      tries are arranged alphabetically. Title and author indexes.

                              DICTIONARIES

522. American Medical Association. Committee on the Medical Aspects of
      Sports. Subcommittee on Classification of Sports Injuries.
      Standard Nomenclature of Athletic Injuries. Chicago, IL: The
      Association, 1976. 157 p. LC 67-1151.

      Provides a definitive language for uniform and meaningful reporting
      of injuries that occur in athletics. Includes synonym, etiology,
      symptoms, physical findings, complications, laboratory and x-ray
      data. Reprint of 1966 edition.

523. Hoover, Richard L., Thomas Fagan, and Ronald O'Neil. A - Z Guide
      to Athletic Injuries. 1st ed. n.p.: Beta Publishing, 1978.
      78 p.

      Apart from the A - Z arrangement of terms with their diagnosis and
      treatment, this guide also has separate sections on standard proce-
      dures for sprains, bone contusions, pulled muscles, etc. Other
      features include glossaries of surgical terms, terms for inservice
      sports medicine, common prefixes, root words, etc. These useful
      sections could do with a subject index.

                    DIRECTORIES AND LOCATIONAL SOURCES

524. Shaw, P., ed. Sport Medicine Directory. 2nd ed. Ottawa, ONT:
      Sport Medicine Council of Canada, 1982. 345 p. index.

Arranged by province, then city, this source identifies athletic
therapists, physicians, physiotherapists, and sports scientists in
Canada who have interests/expertise in medical aspects of sport.
Also includes a clinic registry, listing of foreign practitioners
and clinics (including U. S.), and an index of practitioners according to sport interest.

525. Taking Action for Fitness: A Guide to Selected Information Re-
      sources. Washington, DC: Office of Health Information, Health
      Promotion and Physical Fitness and Sports Medicine, Dept. of
      Health and Human Services, 1981. 24 p. LC 81-50164.

Section 1 lists alphabetically 15 different sports activities and
identifies either an organization and its purposes, information
services and publications, or a few publications with ordering information that provide information about the physical fitness aspects of the sport. Section 2 lists general organizations that
cover a range of sports, and section 3 lists organizations ad-
dressed to fitness concerns for special groups.

ENCYCLOPEDIAS

526. American College of Sports Medicine, University of Wisconsin. En-
      cyclopedia of Sport Sciences and Medicine. New York: Macmillan,
      1971. 1707 p. illus. index. LC 70-87898.

This reputable source provides comprehensive treatment of sport
medicine in 10 basic areas, ranging from physical activity, environment, drugs, to prevention of injuries and rehabilitation. Signed
articles deal with specific aspects of each area, complete with
bibliographic references. Certain chapters, such as injury and
safety devices, have sub-divisions by sports. Extensive subject
and author indexes. A standard source.

527. Kuntzleman, Charles T., ed. Physical Fitness Encyclopedia. Emmaus,
      PA: Rodale Books, 1970. 582 p. illus. bibl. LC 76-116512.

Emphasis is on bio-medical and physiological aspects of physical
fitness. Dictionary arrangement of brief to six-page entries.
Somewhat dated, especially regarding women and girls' participation
in physical fitness and sports activities. Many useful charts and
tables.

528. Midgley, Ruth, et al. The Complete Encyclopedia of Exercises. New
      York: Van Nostrand Reinhold Co., 1981. 335 p. illus. bibl.
      LC 80-51138.

One of the Diagram Group's publications, this covers 350 exercises
of every type from jogging to bodybuilding, and for children as
well as for the elderly. First three of the eight chapters explain
the body function, reasons for different exercises and an assessment of a fit body. Each exercise is laid out in steps and illustrated with diagrams. Subject index provides access by sports.

529. Ryan, Allan J., and Fred L. Allman, Jr., eds. Sports Medicine.
      New York: Academic Press, 1974. 735 p. illus. index. LC 72-
      82639.

      Edited by two M.D.'s, this source covers nutrition, immediate man-
      agement of injuries, rehabilitation, examination and exercise-re-
      lated diseases. Author and subject indexes.

530. Sheehan, George. Encyclopedia of Athletic Medicine. Mountain View,
      CA: Anderson World, 1980. 96 p. illus. index. LC 80-24113.

      A runner's guide to ailments and treatments. Articles are cate-
      gorized into structural problems, internal problems, environmental
      problems. Subject index. Author claims that his advice is "uncon-
      ventional by established medical standards."

531. Southmayd, William, and Marshall Hoffman. Sports Health - The Com-
      plete Book of Athletic Injuries. New York: Quick Fox, 1981.
      459 p. illus. bibl. index. LC 81-50613.

      An extremely informative and useful reference book on injuries, or-
      ganized into 20 sections by body parts. For each type of injury
      (e.g. wrist, shoulder, head, etc.) a chart is provided indicating
      the percent of the particular injury per sport as compared to the
      total number of injuries sustained in the particular sport. De-
      tailed description of anatomy, injury diagnosis and surgical treat-
      ment.

OTHER

532. American Alliance for Health, Physical Education, and Recreation.
      Nutrition for Athletes: A Handbook for Coaches. Washington, DC:
      AAHPER, 1978. 56 p. illus.

      Provides recommendations for nutritional needs of athletes during
      training and performances, with extensive use of charts and tables.
      The data on energy expenditures for various sports are particularly
      useful. No index.

533. Williams, J. G. P. Color Atlas of Injury in Sport. Chicago, IL:
      Year Book Medical Publishers, 1980. 152 p. illus. bibl. in-
      dex. LC 80-156757.

      Color and x-rays photos of injuries with a legend for each to iden-
      tify the sport, e.g. tennis elbow, patella tendonitis in jumper's
      knee, etc. Extremely useful for physicians and athletes. Subject
      index.

PSYCHOLOGICAL, SOCIOLOGICAL, AND PHILOSOPHICAL ASPECTS

534.   Annotated Bibliography on Perceptual-Motor Development. Washington, DC: American Alliance for Health, Physical Education and Recreation, 1973. 115 p. LC 73-160756.

Provides informative annotations for articles, books and audio-visual materials. Arranged by author, the three sections cover works of five prominent researchers, works in seven broad subjects, and films, tests and assessment of perceptual-motor programs. Includes a list of publishers.

535.   Burdge, Rabel J., et al. A Social Science Bibliography of Leisure and Recreation Research. Lexington, KY: University of Kentucky, College of Agriculture, 1975. 112 p. (ERIC ED 137 283).

Topics covered include philosophical issues in leisure, theories, and methods in leisure and recreation research, economic and business aspects of leisure, sports, and profiles of leisure and recreation behavior.

536.   Hammer, Bill. Bibliography of References of the Psychological Aspects of Men and Women in Sports. Santa Barbara, CA: University of California, 1975. 57 p. index.

This bibliography is a poorly typed in-house publication of over 600 articles and dissertations. It's arranged into separate sections for men and women. Each section begins with a subject index with references to citations that are in alphabetical order.

537.   Luschen, Gunther R. F., and George H. Sage, eds. Handbook of Social Sciences of Sport, with an International Classified Bibliography. Champaign, IL: Stipes Pub. Co., 1981. 720 p. LC 80-54273.

A thorough and basic source for background and references to the international literature of the sociology and psychology of sport. (Based on 1982 secondary source.)

538. Salmela, John H. The World Sport Psychology Sourcebook. Ithaca,
        NY: Mouvement Publications, 1981. 423 p. illus. bibl. index.

        A result of a survey of the professional status of sport psychology
        in the world. Arranged in 3 parts, it answers questions on sport
        psychology, documents countries' status by regions, and identifies
        who's who in sport psychology. Comparative tables are given in
        Part I that highlight the findings of countries' status. Keyword
        index. Appendixes include ethical principles for research in sport
        psychology.

539. Social Sciences of Sport: Bibliographies on Educational Topics
        No. 3. Washington, DC: ERIC Clearinghouse on Teacher Education,
        1976. 71 p. (ERIC ED 128 293).

        Annotated bibliography in four sections of ERIC documents and jour-
        nal articles covering sport history, sport psychology, sport so-
        ciology, and sport philosophy.

540. Thomas, Carolyn E., et al. Bibliography: Philosophy of Sport.
        Athens, OH: Philosophic Society for the Study of Sport. Ohio
        University, Department of Philosophy, 1978. 37 p.

        This is a mimeographed listing arranged by author of English and
        foreign monographs, journal articles, and unpublished material on
        all aspects of the philosophy of sport.

SPORTS INDUSTRY

541. Desk Reference Directory. Collingwood, ONT: Jim Rennie's Sports
     Letter. Annual. 1979-   .

     Provides directory-type information for Canadian sources of sport-
     ing goods and ski equipment, clothing and footwear. Arranged in
     three main sections: suppliers, suppliers by product categories,
     and brand names. In English and French. (1982 ed. examined.)

542. NSGA Buying Guide. Chicago, IL: National Sporting Goods Associa-
     tion. Annual. 19?-   .

     Lists manufacturers of sporting goods, sales agents, trade associa-
     tions, and sports service organizations. (Based on 1980 secondary
     source.)

543. Nationwide Directory Sporting Goods Buyer. New York: Salesman's
     Guide, Inc. Annual. 19?-   . ISSN 0148-2734.

     Lists 4,700 retail stores with sales in excess of $100,000. Sport-
     ing goods include equipment, apparel and footwear. Companies are
     arranged by states, with names of buyers, managers, presidents, and
     sales volumes. An alphabetical index of all firms is provided.
     (Based on 1980 secondary source.)

544. Sporting Goods Directory. St. Louis, MO: The Sporting Goods
     Dealers. Annual. 1913?-   .

     Main part is a list of suppliers organized first by sport, then by
     sporting goods product. Indexes for products and advertisers.
     Separate alphabetical listings of suppliers' names and addresses
     and manufacturing agents, wholesalers, and trade associations/or-
     ganizations complete this source. (Continues Sporting Goods Trade
     Directory.) (1980 ed. examined.)

545. Sporting Goods Register. St. Louis, MO: Sporting Goods Dealer.
     Annual. 19?-   . ISSN 0363-1478.

A directory of wholesalers, manufacturers' agents, and importers
of sporting goods, arranged alphabetically by states, and by cities
within states. Information on firms gives address, phone number,
net worth, buyers, sport items, territory, number of salesmen, and
whether catalog available. Trade organizations' address and officials are included. (Based on 1980 secondary source.)

546. Sportsguide for Individual Sports. Ed. by Richard A. Lipsey. New
     York: Sportsguide Inc. Annual. 1980-   . index. ISSN 0198-
     9987.

A companion to Sportsguide for Team Sports (#547), this guide contains listings for all major organizations serving 14 individual
sports from alpine skiing to tennis. Apart from histories, publications and schedules, a major section is the master manufacturers'
directory. Index of organizations. (1980 ed. examined.)

547. Sportsguide for Team Sports. Ed. by Richard A. Lipsey. New York:
     Sportsguide Inc. Annual. 1980-   . bibl. index. ISSN 0198-
     8190.

This is a combination of directory and consumer guide to U. S. and
Canadian team sports markets, covering suppliers, associations,
leagues, conferences, broadcasting media, periodicals, etc. Also
includes a schedule of major events for the year, and sport histories. (1980 ed. examined.)

548. Sportsguide Master Reference. Princeton, NJ: Sportsguide Inc.
     Annual. 1981-   . ISSN 0277-0296.

This source has been formed by the union of Sportsguide for Individual Sports (#546) and Sportsguide for Team Sports (#547).
(Based on 1982 secondary source.)

PART III
INDEXES, DATA BASES, AND INFORMATION CENTERS

32.
PERIODICAL INDEXING/ ABSTRACTING SERVICES AND COMPUTERIZED BIBLIOGRAPHIC DATA BASES

Prior to 1978, only three major sources indexed physical education and sport information: an annual bibliography published by the American Alliance for Health, Physical Education, Recreation and Dance, the Education Index, and Readers' Guide to Periodical Literature. The rest of the physical education periodical literature was scattered throughout the resources of such disciplines as medical sciences, sociology, psychology, and women's studies. Recognition of the field as a separate disciplinary study increased as attention was focused on physical fitness at special White House conferences. By the late 1970's a number of new indexes started appearing.

In the area of computerized information storage and retrieval, the Canadians have led the way through the development of data bases in sociology of leisure and sport at the University of Waterloo, and in sport and recreation at the Sport Resource Information Centre in Ottawa. These two centers continue to offer the most comprehensive computerized retrieval systems in their subject areas.

The purpose of this chapter is 1) to identify those indexing/abstracting services whose primary subject focus is sports, physical education and allied fields; 2) to highlight some selective periodical indexes/abstracts that provide limited access to the field; 3) to provide information on the growing number of computerized data bases for automated bibliographic retrieval. Within the annotations, those are indicated with an asterisk (*). Additionally, the scope includes such non-periodical indexes as ERIC and newspaper indexes. Most of the computerized data bases are available from either Lockheed, Bibliographic Retrieval Services, or System Development Corporation, unless otherwise specified. Addresses of vendors are given at the end of Part III.

MAJOR INDEXES/ABSTRACTS

549. Completed Research in Health, Physical Education, and Recreation. Reston, VA: Research Council of the American Alliance for Health, Physical Education, Recreation and Dance. Annual. 1959-   .

Bibliographic index to approximately 168 English language journals and U. S. masters theses and doctoral dissertations. Major emphasis is on the research of physiological and medical aspects of sport. A single subject index in the front.

550. International Sport Sciences. The Franklin Research Center. Philadelphia, PA: The Franklin Institute Press. Monthly. 1979-   .

An abstracting service to the English and foreign-language periodical literature of sports medicine and sports sciences. Arranged by eleven categories with a subject and author index in the back. Lengthy abstracts follow bibliographic citations. Issues also contain a book review section and information on international sport sciences meetings. (Current publishing status unverified).

551. Physical Education Index. Cape Girardeau, MO: Ben Oak Publishing Co. Quarterly. Annual cumulation. 1978-   . ISSN 0191-9202.

Single, dictionary-style subject index to about 177 U. S. and foreign periodicals published in English or with English summaries. Comprehensive coverage for dance, health, physical education, physical therapy, recreation, sports, and sports medicine. Extensive coverage to the periodical literature of biomechanics, kinesiology, coaching, facilities, and the philosophy, psychology and sociology of sport.

552. Physical Education/Sports Index. Albany, NY: Marathon Press. Quarterly. Annual cumulation. 1978-   . ISSN 0162-007X.

A two part subject index to about 120 U. S. and foreign periodicals published in English or with English summaries. Part one provides subject access for journals in physical education, recreation and allied fields such as sports medicine. Part two provides coverage by specific sports and activities. (Current publishing status unverified).

553. Physical Fitness/Sports Medicine. President's Council on Physical Fitness and Sports. Washington, DC: Government Printing Office. Quarterly. 1978-   . ISSN 0163-2582.

A subject and author index to English-language and foreign-language periodicals that print English abstracts for the areas of exercise physiology, sports injuries, physical conditioning and the medical aspects of exercise. Papers presented at selected congresses are also included. The citations are from the MEDLINE data base of the National Library of Medicine.

* MEDLINE (MEDLARS on Line - Medical Literature Automated Retrieval System) 1966-   .

The whole data base contains over 400,000 citations to articles
from over 3,000 international biomedical journals. Beginning
with 1974, abstracts of articles are also available for searching. Physical Fitness/Sports Medicine represents those citations
from the data base pertaining to the particular subject area.
The terms used are from Medical Subject Headings (MeSH) list, and
correspond to those used in Index Medicus, which is the print
counterpart of the data base.

554. Runner's Index. Ed. by Joseph C. Mancuso. Waco, TX: Joseph C.
      Mancuso. Semi-annual. 1978-   .

A three part index to English-language scholarly and popular journals for all aspects of running. The first and main part provides
subject access to journal articles. The second part is an author
index, and the third part is an index to races arranged by title
and/or location of race.

555. Sociology of Leisure and Sport Abstracts. Amsterdam, The Nether-
      lands; New York: Elsevier Scientific. Triannual. Index cumu-
      lates annually. 1980-   .

A continuation of SIRLS standard files (#555* following) in a single source. Citations arranged by accession numbers with a subject
and author index.

   * SIRLS data base. Waterloo, ONT: University of Waterloo, Facul-
      ty of Human Kinetics and Leisure Studies. 1963-   .

      A computerized information retrieval system for the sociology
      of leisure and sport. International coverage of journals in
      English and foreign languages, conference proceedings, unpub-
      lished papers, theses, monographs and government publications.
      Scope also includes the social, economic, and political aspects
      of sport, cultural development, anthropology, and history. The
      data base consists of over 16,000 references with abstracts,
      most of which are available from the Faculty of Human Kinetics
      in either hard copy or microfiche. Approximately 1,000 cita-
      tions are added annually. Forty-three standard print files were
      generated with annual updates, each pertaining to an area of re-
      search, such as "Personality and Sport. File no. 29." These
      files were discontinued in 1979 with the commercial publication
      of Sociology of Leisure and Sport Abstracts (#555). The depart-
      ment handles computer search requests, as this data base is not
      available through any U. S. vendors.

556. Sport and Recreation Index. Ottawa, ONT: Sport Information Re-
      source Centre. Monthly. 1977-   . ISSN 0705-6095.

Bilingual index with a "General Topics" section and a "Sports" section. Selectively covers approximately 675 English and foreign-
language journals. Emphasis is on research articles and those of
interest to practitioners. A table of contents serves as the subject index. (Formerly Sport Articles v. 1 - 4, 1974-77.)

* SIRC data base. 1975-   .

This data base contains over 90,000 citations of books, periodical articles, theses, microforms, and conference proceedings.
Most of these are in English and French. The Centre also keeps
print copies of most documents, and each has a specific number
for identification. Sport Bibliography (#366) is a print product of the data base, and cumulates Sport and Recreation Index
up through 1980. SIRC provides computer searching and document
delivery.

SELECTED SUPPLEMENTARY INDEXES/ABSTRACTS

557. America: History and Life. Santa Barbara, CA: American Bibliographical Center of ABC-Clio, Inc. 1964-   .

Provides coverage to U. S. and Canada's literature on history and
social conditions. Articles and books on sports history research
listed under the terms "sports," "games," "outdoor life," etc. Or-
ganized in 4 parts:
Part A - triannual - article abstracts/citations. ISSN 0002-7065.
Part B - semi-annual - book reviews. ISSN 0097-6172.
Part C - annual - American history bibliography.
Part D - annual index.

* America: History and Life data base. 1964-   .

This file contains over 90,000 citations and abstracts from 1,900
foreign and domestic journals and 2,400 other sources. Updates
quarterly with 11,000 additional records per year. It also includes appropriate citations from Dissertation Abstracts International (#563).

558. Biography Index. Bronx, NY: H. W. Wilson Co. Quarterly. Annual
cumulation. 1946-   . ISSN 0006-3053.

A comprehensive name index to biographical materials from 700
periodicals, books, obituaries, diaries, memoirs, letters. There
is a list of biographees organied by profession.

559. Business Periodicals Index. Bronx, NY: W. H. Wilson Co. Monthly.
Annual cumulation. 1958-   . ISSN 0007-6961.

Indexes magazine articles that explore the economics of sports,
games, health clubs, TV sports advertising, etc.

560. Canadian News Index. Toronto, ONT: Micromedia Ltd. Monthly.
Annual cumulation. 1977-   . ISSN 0384-983X.

An index to seven of the most important English-language Canadian newspapers: Calgary Herald, Vancouver Sun, Globe & Mail, Winnipeg Free Press, Montreal Gazette, Halifax Chronicle Herald, and Toronto Star. Subject areas covered include news on international, national and provincial affairs, editorials, government activities, book reviews, biographies and sports. The subject index includes names of organizations and government agencies with a separate biography index section. Each entry is enriched to enhance information content, and is chronologically arranged.

* Canadian News Index data base. 1977-   .

Developed in 1977, this file increases at an annual rate of approximately 72,000 records. Micromedia Ltd. provides on-line searching of this data base.

561. Canadian Periodical Index. Ottawa, ONT: Canadian Library Association. Monthly. Annual cumulation. 1938-   . ISSN 0008-4719.

This bilingual source indexes close to 100 Canadian periodicals, none of which are strictly sports journals, however. Entries in English or French are listed under "sports," "athletes," and names of sports, with topical subheadings. A list of related headings is given under "sports."

562. Current Index to Journals in Education. Phoenix, AZ: Oryx Press. Monthly. Annual cumulation. 1969-   . ISSN 0098-0897.

A monthly index to articles published in approximately 780 major educational and education-related journals. A companion to Resources in Education (#572), it is part of a family of reference publications sponsored by the Educational Resources Information Center (ERIC). It uses the same controlled vocabulary as RIE, called Thesaurus of ERIC Descriptors. Individual sport names are listed as subject terms, with the majority of sports related literature posted under "Physical Education." Subject index, author index, and journal content index.

* ERIC data base. 1966-   .

(see #572*)

563. Dissertation Abstracts International. Ann Arbor, MI: University Microfilms International. Monthly. Annual author index. 1938-   . ISSN 0419-4209   ISSN 0419-4217

A monthly compilation of abstracts of doctoral dissertations from American, Canadian, and selected international universities. Each monthly publication comes in two separate issues: A - The Humanities and Social Sciences, and B - The Sciences and Engineering. The main sections of both issues are further divided into five different fields of study, e.g. education, physical sciences, etc. A keyword title index provides multiple subject access. Author index cumulates annually. Copies of complete texts, with a few exceptions, are available for purchase as microfilms or as xerographic prints from University Microfilms.

* Comprehensive Dissertation Index data base. 1861-   .

This data base of over 700,000 citations is the counterpart of
three printed publications by the University Microfilms: Dissertation Abstracts International, American Doctoral Dissertations
and Comprehensive Dissertation Index; the latter provides subject
access to the first two. Apart from subject, author, and title,
the searchable items include names of institutions, a feature
lacking from the printed sources. Abstracts are non-searchable
items. University Microfilms also handles computer search requests.

564. Education Index. Bronx, NY: H. W. Wilson Co. Monthly. Annual
      cumulation. 1929-   . ISSN 0013-1385.

A cumulative author/subject index to over 300 U. S. journals and a
few foreign ones in the English language. Approximately 10 of
these titles are physical education journals. It provides excellent subject access by individual sports, "physical education for
girls and women," "physical education facilities," "sports and
society," etc. with as many as 28 specific topical subheadings such
as "history," "equipment," "curriculum," "elementary schools," etc.
or subdivisions by countries.

565. Exceptional Child Education Resources. Reston, VA: Council for
      Exceptional Children. Quarterly. Index cumulates annually.
      1969-   . ISSN 0160-4309.

An abstracting source to journal articles, books, dissertations,
non-print media, curriculum guides, legislative documents, etc. on
gifted and handicapped children. Particularly useful in researching literature on adapted physical education.

* ECER data base. 1966-   .

This data base contains over 37,000 citations and abstracts and
expands at the rate of around 750 records per quarter. Roughly
one fourth of these citations are duplicated in ERIC (#572*),
and can be excluded from a computer search if specified.

566. Magazine Index. Menlo Park, CA: Information Access Corporation.
      Monthly. Monthly cumulation for latest 4 yrs. 1977-   .

A 16mm computer output microfilm index to over 370 popular magazines, including all those covered in Readers' Guide (#571). Approximately 30 of these magazines are entirely sports related, providing extensive coverage on sports, travel, recreation, etc. Uses
Library of Congress Subject Headings in addition to commonly used
terms.

* Magazine Index data base. 1977-   .

Essentially a data file of over 300,000 citations available from
Readers' Guide as well as from other magazines. It is updated
monthly with 10,000 records per update. Some titles of articles
are annotated and their keywords are also available for searching.

567. Monthly Catalog of U. S. Government Publications. Washington, DC:
Government Printing Office. Monthly. Index cumulates annually.
1900-   . ISSN 0362-6830.

A comprehensive list to all federal government agency publications,
Congressional hearings and reports, with keyword, title, subject
and author indexes. Materials on sports primarily reflect health,
physical fitness and recreational outdoor sports topics.

* GPO Monthly Catalog data base. 1976-   .

This machine-readable equivalent of the printed Monthly Catalog
contains over 75,000 records with monthly updates. The Superintendent of Documents numbers are provided with each citation.
Each issue of serials has its own entry, resulting in multiple
listing of the same title.

568. National Newspaper Index. Menlo Park, CA: Information Access Corporation. Monthly. 1979-   .

This 16mm microfilm index provides comprehensive coverage to the
Christian Science Monitor, New York Times, and the Wall Street Journal, with the exception of weather charts, stock market tables,
crossword puzzles, and horoscopes. Uses Library of Congress Subject headings. New York Times is an excellent information source
on various national league games.

* National Newspaper Index data base. 1979-   .

With over 200,000 records, this data base is useful for factual
reference questions on issues of contemporary national interest
such as economy, government policies, foreign relations and
sports.

* Newsearch data base. Current month only.

This is a daily update of over 1,500 news stories, book reviews,
articles from nearly 500 of the most important periodicals,
magazines, and newspapers. At the end of each month, citations
from newspapers and periodicals/magazines are transferred to the
National Newspaper Index data base, and the Magazine Index data
base, respectively. It is virtually an up-to-date record of
those 2 files.

569. Philosopher's Index. Bowling Green, OH: Philosophy Documentation
Center. Quarterly. Annual cumulation. 1967-   . ISSN 0031-7993.

An abstracting source to over 400 scholarly journals in English, French, German, Spanish, and Italian with subject and author indexes. Separate book review index in the back. Materials on philosophy of sports are indexed under "athletics" or "sports."

* Philosopher's Index data base. 1940-   .

This file contains over 70,000 records with quarterly updates of 1,500. Since subject access for sport is limited to the 2 terms "Athletics" and "Sports," free text searching to include title and abstracts is essential for the retrieval of references on more specific aspects of sport philosophy, e.g. pursuit of bodily excellence, Weiss theory, freedom and sports, etc.

570. Psychological Abstracts. Arlington, VA: American Psychological Association, Inc. Monthly. Index cumulates annually. 1927-   . ISSN 0033-2887.

A major abstracting service to the world periodical literature in psychology and related disciplines. Extensive coverage on sports psychology, such as aggression, winning, performance, etc. Some relevant terms are names of sports, "physical fitness," "recreation," "physical education," etc.

* PsyINFO data base. 1967-   .

A data file of 350,000 citations and abstracts with 2,500 per month updates. Although the print index is generated from the data file, citations to books and dissertations can only be retrieved through computer searching. Uses controlled vocabulary given in the Thesaurus of Psychological Index Terms, which is available on-line if searching the data base on Lockheed's DIALOG.

571. Readers' Guide to Periodical Literature. Bronx, NY: H. W. Wilson Co. Semi-monthly. Annual cumulation. 1890-   . ISSN 0034-2887.

A dictionary subject index to popular magazine articles. Sports Illustrated is the major source for sport literature comprehensively indexed by Readers' Guide. Excellent subject access via any sport names, league, players, teams, etc.

* Magazine Index data base. 1977-   .

(see #566*)

572. Resources in Education. Educational Resources Information Center, U. S. Department of Education, National Institute of Education. Washington, DC: Government Printing Office. Monthly. Index cumulates annually. 1966-   . ISSN 0098-0897.

A monthly abstracting service to published/unpublished research reports, government documents, curriculum guides, conference proceedings, and dissertations relating to education. Most documents are
available on microfiche. Subject index, author index, institution
index and publication type index. Three microfiche indexes: RIE
identifiers Usage Report 1967-   , RIE Descriptors Usage Report
1967-   , Author index 1966-   cumulate all citations by the ED
numbers under identifiers, descriptors and authors, respectively.
Particularly useful is the usage report for identifiers (such as
names of tests, names of programs) which provides an extra means
of access in manual searching of the sources. Such usage reports
also are available for CIJE (#562).

* ERIC data base. 1966-   .

  Provides computerized access to over 295,000 citations and abstracts in both Resources in Education and Current Index to
  Journal in Education (#562). Updates monthly with approximately
  3,000 citations. The controlled vocabulary is given in the Thesaurus of ERIC Descriptors which indicates the number of postings
  of CIJE and RIE citations for each term. Identifiers, which are
  not provided in the print index but are available on the microfiche usage report, and abstracts are two other searchable elements in addition to descriptors, authors and titles. RIE citations could be retrieved separately from CIJE's if so specified.

573.   Social Sciences Citation Index. Philadelphia, PA: Institute for
       Scientific Information. Triannual. Annual cumulation.
       1973-   . ISSN 0091-3707.

A multidisciplinary index of 1,000 of the most important social and
behavioral science journals throughout the world. It also includes
social science articles selected from over 2,000 journals in the
natural, physical and biomedical sciences. Citation indexing provides a means of identifying authors with the same areas of research
interest. Part I - citation index; Part II - source index, corporate address index, permuterm subject index.

* Social Scisearch data base. 1972-   .

  This data base of over 800,000 records with monthly updates offers a unique information retrieval technique. In addition to
  more conventional method of searching title, author, subject,
  journal names, etc., it provides access by author's cited references. The Institute for Scientific Information also accepts
  search requests as well as providing document delivery.

574.   Sociological Abstracts. San Diego, CA: Sociological Abstracts,
       Inc. 5 issues a year. Index cumulates annually. 1953-   .
       ISSN 0038-0202.

A comprehensive index to the world's periodical literature in sociology and related disciplines in the social and behavioral sciences. Over 1,200 journals in more than 30 languages are scanned
for inclusion. Apart from the cumulative subject, author, and index of authors of book reviews, there is a cumulative journal
source index. This lists all indexed serial titles with addresses
of their publishers, title changes, and/or expiration dates. This
source index also serves as a kind of "table of contents" to identify coverage of various journal issues in Sociological Abstracts.
Most of the articles on sociology of sports can be located under
the terms "recreation" and "leisure."

* Sociological Abstracts data base. 1963-   .

Consists of over 100,000 citations, with 5 updates a year adding
1,500 new records each update. Sociological Abstracts, Inc. also provides on-line computer searching of this data base and re-
production and document delivery service.

575.   Women Studies Abstracts. Rush, NY: Women Studies Abstracts.
       Quarterly. Annual index. 1972-   . ISSN 0049-7835.

This major abstracting service to research relating to aspects of
women studies covers over 380 journals, basically published in
United States, Canada and Britain. Access to sports related articles is provided via individual sport terms. A useful source for
researching sex roles and stereotyping in sports.

ADDRESSES OF ON-LINE VENDORS

Bibliographic Retrieval Service, Inc.
   Route 7
   Latham, NY 12110

Infomart
   One Yonge Street, Suite 1506
   Toronto, Ontario
   Canada M4E 1E5

Lockheed Information Systems
   Organization 5208, Building 201
   3251 Hanover Street
   Palo Alto, CA 94304

Micromedia Ltd.
   144 Front Street West
   Toronto, Ontario
   Canada M5G 2L7

System Development Corp. Search Services
   2500 Colorado Avenue
   Santa Monica, CA 90406

33.
INFORMATION/DOCUMENTATION CENTERS AND SPECIAL COLLECTIONS

The following organizations represent U. S. and Canadian information/documentation centers and libraries that maintain special collections of information resources in the areas of sports, physical education, and allied fields. Those organizations with collections exclusively dedicated to recreation and leisure are not included. Organizations were selected for inclusion if they met the following criteria: 1) the collection of sports and/or physical education information resources; 2) the provision of information services to user groups other than just their members or primary user population.

While there are many other athletic and sports organizations that maintain biographical archives and statistical data records; offer film services; or sponsor educational and research activities through their committee undertakings, they have not been included here unless they also maintain collections of information resources available for research or general use and provide minimal information services to users. The reader is encouraged to consult the following sources for information regarding such excluded organizations: Encyclopedia of Associations. 3 vols. 17th ed. Detroit MI: Gale, 1982; Directory of Special Libraries and Information Centers. 6th ed. Detroit, MI: Gale, 1981.

Sports and physical education collections housed in university or public libraries have been included in this section if the size of the collection was at least 500 volumes and if a particular sports or allied field emphasis or specialization is represented in the collection. Collections containing only manuscripts were excluded, however. The reader is encouraged to consult: Ash, Lee, comp. Subject Collections. 5th rev. and enlarged ed. New York: Bowker, 1978, in order to identify those specialized collections not included here.

We also excluded those research centers primarily dedicated to sponsoring or carrying out research studies in the areas of sports and physical education. To identify such organizations the reader should consult The Research Centers Directory. 7th ed. Detroit, MI: Gale, 1982.

Public access varies from organization to organization. The reader can assume that access is open to the public unless stated otherwise in the description under each entry.

Although efforts were made to obtain current addresses, telephone numbers, and names of contact persons, not all organizations responded to a mail questionnaire.

The arrangement is in two sections: 1) organizations with collections devoted to a particular sport; and 2) organizations with collections covering sports, physical education or an allied field.

INDIVIDUAL SPORTS

576. Charles W. Mears BASEBALL Collection
      Cleveland Public Library - Fine Arts Dept.
      325 Superior Ave., Cleveland, OH 44114
      (216) 623-2848
      Contact person: Head, Fine Arts Dept.

      Purpose: To collect, maintain, and make available a collection of
      over 2,000 books and magazines, and newspapers from the late 1800's
      on baseball.

      Services: Reference assistance provided for in person, telephone
      or mail inquiries; copying and interlibrary loan services.

577. National BASEBALL Hall of Fame and Museum, National Baseball Library
      Main St., Cooperstown, NY 13326
      (607) 547-9988
      Contact person: John Redding, Librarian
      Founded: 1968

      Purpose: To support the service objectives of the Hall of Fame and
      Museum by maintaining a collection of about 4,400 books, 8 periodi-
      cal subscriptions, audio-visual materials, clippings files, photo-
      graphs, etc. Special collections include the August Herrmann cor-
      respondence, A. G. Mills correspondence, and official records of
      the major leagues.

      Services: Reference assistance for in person, telephone and mail
      inquiries; allow in-house use of collection; and provide copying
      facilities.

      Access: By appointment only.

      Note: Informal affiliation exists between the library and the So-
      ciety for American Baseball Research, P. O. Box 323, Cooperstown,
      NY 13326, (607) 547-8728. This organization's purpose is to fos-
      ter the study of baseball and to coordinate and facilitate the dis-
      semination of baseball research information.

578. Naismith Memorial BASKETBALL Hall of Fame
      460 Alden St., Springfield, MA 01109
      (413) 781-6500
      Contact person: Lee Williams, Executive Director

      Purpose: To present the Naismith and Bunn Awards annually and to
      maintain the Hall of Fame and Library.

      Services: Maintains the Edward J. and Gena Hickox Library contain-
      ing 1,600 volumes on basketball and related subjects; allow in-
      house use of collection.

      Publications: Newsletter (quarterly).

      Access: Open by appointment only.

579. (BOATING)
Aquatic Hall of Fame and Museum of Canada, Library
25 Poseidon Bay, Winnipeg, Man., Canada R3M 3E4
(204) 947-0131

Purpose: To collect and maintain a collection of materials to support the service requirements for the Hall of Fame and Museum.
Collection of library materials includes: record books, books from
the Cutty Sark Club of Winnipeg, and a variety of materials for the
sports of swimming, diving, water polo, sailing, and yachting.

Services: Limited reference assistance provided for mail and telephone inquiries.

Access: By appointment.

580. (BOATING)
State University of New York Maritime College, Stephen B. Luce
    Library
Fort Schuyler, Bronx, NY   10465
(212) 892-3004, Ext. 235
Contact person: Richard H. Corson, Librarian

Purpose: To collect, maintain, and make available an extensive
collection of books, periodicals, maps, pictures, and audio-visual
materials on maritime sciences.

Services: Reference assistance provided for in person, telephone
or mail inquiries; allow in-house use of collection; provide copying and interlibrary loan services.

581. (EQUESTRIAN)
Jockey Club
P. O. Box 22580, Lexington, KY   40522
(606) 269-5602
Contact person: William H. Anderson

Purpose: Maintains a data base of information on horse pedigrees,
racing and breeding records.

Services: The Kentucky office provides reference assistance for
members and serious researchers by making available their computerized system for searching their data base. The New York office
(Jockey Club, 380 Madison Avenue, NY, NY   10017, (212) 599-1919)
maintains the breed registry and publishes the American Stud Book
(every 4 years). This collection consists of stud books and racing
calendars.

Access: Members and serious researchers by appointment only.

582.   (EQUESTRIAN)
Keeneland Association Library
Keeneland Race Course, Box 1690, Lexington, KY 40592
(606) 254-3412
Contact person: Doris J. Waren, Librarian
Founded: 1939

Purpose: To collect, maintain and provide service to the public
through a comprehensive library of thoroughbred horse racing and
breeding and horse sports materials. Collection consists of about
5,500 books, 1,100 bound periodical volumes, 200,000 photographic
negatives of American racing, clippings, and pamphlets.

Services: Provides reference services for in person, mail or telephone inquiries; allows in-house use of the collection; and provides facilities for photocopying. A separately published guide to
the collection exists: Buckley, Amelia K. The Keeneland Association Library: Guide to the Collection. Lexington, KY: University
of Kentucky Press, 1958.

583.   (EQUESTRIAN)
National Sporting Library
P. O. Box 1335, Middleburg, VA 22117
(703) 687-6542
Contact person: A. Mackay-Smith, Curator
Founded: 1954

Purpose: To collect, maintain, and make available to the public a
collection of over 11,000 books, periodicals, microfilm, etc. on
thoroughbred racing, breeding, polo, horse shows and allied activities. Special collections consist of the Thomas Holden White Polo
Collection and the Huth-Lonsdale-Arundel Collection of 16th - 19th
century books on horses.

Services: Provide research assistance for in person, mail, or
telephone inquiries; allow in-house use of collection; and provide
photocopying service.

Publications: National Sporting Library Newsletter (biannual) and
the special indexes to N. Y. Sporting Magazine, U. S. Sporting
Magazine, Spirit of the Times, and the American Turf Register.

584.   (EQUESTRIAN)
Prince George's County Memorial Library System, Bowie Branch Library
Selima Room, 15210 Annapolis Rd., Bowie, MD 20715
(301) 262-7000
Contact person: Branch Librarian

Purpose: To collect, maintain, and make available a collection of
about 2,500 items (including pictures), on horses. Emphasis is on
horse-racing and breeding, particularly as it pertains to Maryland.

Services: Reference assistance available for in person, telephone
or mail inquiries; allow in-house use of collection; provide copying and interlibrary loan services. A bibliography of the collection has been prepared by the library staff.

585.   (EQUESTRIAN)
        Trotting Horse Museum, Peter D. Haughton Library
        240 Main St., Goshen, NY 10924
        (914) 294-6330
        Contact person: Philip Pines, Director
        Founded: 1951

        Purpose: To collect and maintain materials on harness racing,
        standard bred horse training, etc. and provide research support
        for the Trotting Horse Museum (Hall of Fame of the Trotter). Col-
        lection consists of over 450 books; 200 bound periodical volumes;
        4,500 record books, sale catalogs and racing records; and motion
        picture films.

        Services: Allow in-house use of the library; provide some re-
        search assistance; and offer educational programs on an irregular
        basis.

        Publications: Newsletter.

        Access: By appointment only.

586.   Pro FOOTBALL Hall of Fame, Library/Research Center
        2121 Harrison Ave., N. W., Canton, OH 44708
        (216) 456-8207
        Contact person: Anne Mannot, Librarian
        Founded: 1963

        Purpose: To support the research needs of the Pro Football Hall of
        Fame staff. To collect, organize, and make available football ma-
        terials to serious researchers and writers. Collection consists
        of 2,060 books, 552 bound periodicals, 500 media guides, 5,000
        programs, 20,000 photographs, 3,000 microfilms, and numerous
        pamphlets.

        Services: Reference assistance for in person, mail or telephone in-
        quiries; allow in-house use of the collection; provide photocopying
        service.

        Access: Serious researchers and writers by appointment only.

        Note: Indirectly affiliated with the Professional Football Re-
        searchers Association, 218 Wise St., N. E., Canton, OH 44720, an
        organization dedicated to fostering the study of professional foot-
        ball.

587.   Canadian GOLF Museum, Library
        Alymer East, Quebec
        Correspondence: 1962 Lauder Dr., Ottawa, Ontario
        Canada K2A 1B1
        (613) 722-9544
        Contact person: W. Lyn Stewart, Curator

Purpose: To collect and maintain sources of information to support the museum's collections. The library collection consists of over 300 books, manuscripts, videotapes, and filmstrips. It contains several old volumes dating from 1875.

Services: Limited reference assistance for in person and mail inquiries; allow in-house use of collection; and provide copying facilities.

Access: By appointment.

588. Professional GOLFER'S Association of America, Library
100 Ave. of the Champions, Palm Beach Gardens, FL 33410
(303) 626-3600
Contact person: Dr. Gary Wiren

Purpose: To provide the most complete research library in the field of golf and to promote a greater interest in golf literature and its writers.

Services: Allow on-site use of a historical collection of early Scottish records dating to 1500's; a large magazine collection; a clippings file; and a 16,000 volume collection on golf; provide limited reference assistance.

Access: Professional Golfer's Association members and others by permission.

589. United States GOLF Association
Golf House, Far Hills, NJ 07931
(201) 234-2300
Contact person: Janet Seagle
Founded: 1894

Purpose: Serves as governing body for golf in the U. S.

Services: Maintains research library of about 8,000 volumes and a picture archive of about 10,000 pictures; provides data on rules, handicapping, amateur status, tournament procedure, turf maintenance, etc.; administers Golf House Museum, a collection of memorabilia; and through the Turfgrass Visiting Service promotes scientific work in green keeping and turf management.

Publications: Golf Journal (8/year), Green Section Record (bi-monthly), plus other handbooks on rules and course maintenance.

590. HOCKEY Hall of Fame, Library
Exhibition Place, Toronto, Ontario
Canada M6K 3C3
(416) 595-1345
Contact person: M. H. (Lefty) Reid, Curator

Purpose: Supports the Hall of Fame displays and exhibits. Hall of Fame displays hockey artifacts and honors the greats of the game.

Services: Maintains about 500 books, 100 bound periodical volumes, 5,000 photographs, 1,000 35mm slides, and scrapbooks. Very limited reference service.

Publications: Hockey's Heritage.

Access: Open to the public by appointment only.

591. American RUNNING and Fitness Association
      2420 K St., N. W., Washington, DC   20037
      (202) 965-3430
      Contact person: Elizabeth Elliott, Executive Director
      Founded: 1968

Purpose: Promotes healthful running; fosters the preventive maintenance concept in health care; and sets standards of performance and safe guidelines for participation.

Services: Serves as a repository of data on running that can be computerized for research purposes; acts as a clearinghouse for questions on running; maintains a library of 2,000 volumes on preventive medicine through exercise; conducts research in exercise physiology and in techniques of increasing total human performance, etc.

Publications: Running and Fitness (bimonthly), Podiatrist Survey (annual), Survey of Exercise Stress Testing Facilities (annual).

592. National SKI Hall of Fame, Roland Palmedo National Ski Library
      P. O. Box 191, Mather Ave., Ishpeming, MI   49849
      (906) 486-9281
      Contact person: Russell M. Magnaghi, Archivist
      Founded: 1978

Purpose: To collect and maintain a collection of materials to support the service and educational needs of the Hall of Fame. The collection includes over 500 book titles, plus audio-visual materials and pamphlets. Particularly strong in the history of skiing.

Publications: Seventy Five Years of Skiing (1904-1979), Skiing Then and Now, Nine Thousand Years of Skis.

Access: By appointment.

593. International SWIMMING Hall of Fame, Museum Library
      One Hall of Fame Drive, Fort Lauderdale, FL   33316
      (305) 462-6536
      Contact person: Marion Washburn, Librarian
      Founded: 1968

Purpose: To support the research needs of the Hall of Fame Museum.
To collect, organize and make available materials related to all
types of aquatic sports with the primary emphasis on swimming, particularly rare and out-of-print editions. Collection consists of
over 2,000 books, 70 bound periodicals, 80 scrapbooks, and miscellaneous materials.

Services: Reference assistance provided for in person, mail or
telephone inquiries; allow in-house use of collection.

594.   Racquet and TENNIS Club Library
        370 Park Ave., New York, NY 10022
        (212) 753-9700
        Contact person: Gerald Belliveau, Librarian
        Founded: 1916

Purpose: To collect, organize, and make available to researchers
a book collection of about 16,500 volumes and a periodical collection of about 45 titles, specializing in court tennis, lawn tennis,
and early American sport.

Services: Provide reference assistance to in person, mail, and
telephone inquiries; allow in-house use of collection; and provide
copying services. A separately published catalog is available (see
#295).

Access: Open to graduate students and researchers by appointment.

595.   United States TENNIS Association, Education and Research Center
        729 Alexander Rd., Princeton, NJ 08540
        (609) 452-2580
        Contact person: Martha T. Wickenden, Coordinator
        Founded: 1972

Purpose: To serve the research and education needs of tennis players, educators, and enthusiasts by acting as a clearinghouse for
tennis information.

Services: Provide replies to mail and telephone inquiries; carry
out research on recreational tennis and publish results in books
and manuals; maintain a publications department of over 75 items
on a wide-ranging list of tennis subjects; and provide film rental
service through the film library; and coordinate local and regional
teacher training workshops.

Publications: Film List (annual) (see #296), plus many other books
and manuals.

596.   William M. Fischer Lawn TENNIS Library, St. John's University
        Grand Central and Utopia Parkways, Jamaica, NY 11439
        (212) 990-6161
        Contact person: Special Collections Librarian

Purpose: To maintain and make available a collection of tennis literature and memorabilia dating from the late 1800's through the early 1950's. It contains a great deal of pamphlets, scrapbook materials, newspaper clippings, and the donor's own records and descriptions of matches and tournaments.

Services: Reference assistance is provided for in person, mail, or telephone inquiries; allow in-house use of the collection.

Access: By appointment.

SPORTS/PHYSICAL EDUCATION AND ALLIED FIELDS

597. Academy for the Psychology of Sports International
2062 Arlington Ave., Toledo, OH 43609
Contact person: William J. Beausay, President
Founded: 1970

Purpose: To advance serious research and increase public understanding of the function of psychology in competitive sports and athletics, and to facilitate communication among organizations and individuals interested in sport psychology.

Services: Serves as a clearinghouse of information for existing and progressing research in the psychology of sports; conducts seminars and clinics; maintains speakers bureau and a library.

598. American Alliance for Health, Physical Education, Recreation and
Dance
Unit on Programs for the Handicapped
1900 Association Dr., Reston, VA 22091
(703) 476-3400
Contact person: Mary Coscarcelli, Librarian
Founded: 1978

Purpose: As part of the AAHPERD, this unit has incorporated some of the functions and services of the former Information and Research Utilization Center for Physical Education for the Handicapped. The Unit on Programs for the Handicapped is the designated information center for the following four inter-association structures of AAHPERD: Adapted Physical Education Academy, Therapeutics Council, Recreation for Special Populations, and Dance for Special Populations. Its purpose is the packaging and dissemination of information on fitness and sports for people of all ages with handicapping conditions.

Services: Provides limited reference and referral assistance for telephone and mail inquiries; carries on an active publishing program; and offers reprint service. Other information services are in the process of being defined.

Publications: Practical Pointers (monthly), Able Bodies (quarterly), Topical Updates and Topical Information Sheets (irregular).

599. American Physical Fitness Research Institute
     824 Moraga Dr., Los Angeles, CA 90049
     (213) 476-6241
     Contact person: Grusha Paterson, Director
     Founded: 1958

     Purpose: To produce, develop and disseminate educational programs
     dealing with a wide variety of physical fitness-related topics.
     To function as a clearinghouse for information on health and fit-
     ness.

     Services: Maintain a 500-volume library; allow in-house use of
     the collection; produce pamphlets, monographs, and educational
     charts.

     Publications: Bulletin (3 times/yr.), Health's-a-Poppin, Educa-
     tor's Guide to Free Tapes (annually).

600. Canada's Sports Hall of Fame, Library
     Exhibition Place, Toronto, Ontario
     Canada M6K 3C3
     (416) 595-1046
     Contact person: J. Thomas West, Director
     Founded: 1955

     Purpose: To preserve and promote Canada's sporting heritage; to
     maintain large display facility open throughout the year; and to
     maintain library of support materials.

     Services: Disseminates sports information and photographs; main-
     tains library, theatre and archives; collects and displays sports
     memorabilia.

     Access: Library available by appointment.

601. Canadian Olympic Association, Library/Information Services Centre
     Olympic House, Cite du Havre
     Montreal, Quebec
     Canada H3C 3E4
     (514) 861-3371
     Contact person: Sylvia Doucette

     Purpose: Maintain the Olympic archive and research centre, which
     specializes in the collection and dissemination of information on
     Olympism and amateur sport.

     Services: Professionally staffed, the Centre distributes print and
     audio-visual materials to sport groups, schools, universities, in-
     dustry, and the media; responds to telephone and mail inquiries;
     maintains a collection of some 1,200 items consisting of books,
     periodicals, reports, conference proceedings, and unpublished do-
     cuments; and operates a film lending library.

     Publications: Information Bulletin, Canada and Olympism, and hand-
     books.

602.   Centre de Documentation en Loisir (Leisure Documentation Center)
       University of Quebec, Trois-Rivieres
       C. P. 500, Trois-Rivieres, Quebec
       Canada G9A 5H7
       (819) 376-5752
       Contact person: Jean-Pierre Biron, Librarian
       Founded: 1975

       Purpose: To collect, organize, and make accessible about 3,000
       books, 250 periodicals, 800 government reports, and 100 audio-vis-
       ual resources on leisure and sport, particularly pertaining to the
       province of Quebec. Sixty percent of the collection is in English
       with the remainder in French.

       Services: Reference assistance provided for in person, mail, or
       telephone inquiries; allow in-house use of the collection; offer
       computerized literature searching and referral and consulting ser-
       vices; and provide material loan services and photocopying facili-
       ties.

603.   Citizens Savings Athletic Foundation
       9800 S. Sepulveda Blvd., Los Angeles, CA   90045
       (213) 670-7550
       Contact person: W. R. Schroeder
       Founded: 1936

       Purpose: To collect, organize, and make accessible one of the most
       extensive collections, particularly for the areas of sports history
       and instruction. To serve as the repository for the Association of
       Sports Museums and Halls of Fame. Collection includes over 10,000
       books; 50 periodical subscriptions; bound volumes of sports sec-
       tions from several newspapers; college and university annuals and
       yearbooks; and souvenir publications from amateur, college, and
       professional sporting events. The holdings of sports records ephe-
       mera and other documentary materials are extremely comprehensive.

       Services: Provides reference assistance for mail or in person in-
       quiries and allows in-house use of the collection.

604.   DePaul University, Library
       The Anita Peabody Sports Collection
       2323 N. Seminary, Chicago, IL 60614
       (312) 321-7934
       Contact person: Special Collections Librarian

       Purpose: To maintain and make available a collection of about 900
       volumes, including about 250 periodical volumes, on various sports.
       Materials cover the middle to late 19th century. Includes a com-
       plete run of The Sporting Magazine, begun in 1792.

       Services: Reference assistance provided for in person, mail, or
       telephone inquiries; allow in-house use of the collection; copying
       services provided and limited interlibrary loan.

605.   ERIC Clearinghouse on Teacher Education
        One Dupont Circle, N. W., Suite 610, Washington, DC   20036
        (202) 293-2450
        Contact person: Dr. Karl Massanari, Director
        Founded: 1966

        Purpose: To identify, obtain, and make available unpublished and
        published documents pertaining to recreation education, health edu-
        cation, physical education (20% of the total documentation effort),
        and on all aspects of teacher education.   The number of documents
        in collection exceeds 34,000.

        Services: Provide in person, mail or telephone reference assis-
        tance; allow in-house use of collection; provide photocopying and
        microfilm/microfiche copying; computerized bibliographic searching
        on-demand; referral services provided; and forward citations and
        abstracts of all material for inclusion in the ERIC computer data
        base.

        Publications: Quarterly Information Bulletin.

606.   Leisure Studies Data Bank, Department of Recreation
        Faculty of Human Kinetics and Leisure Studies, University of
            Waterloo
        Waterloo, Ontario
        Canada   N2L 3G1
        (519) 885-1211, Ext. 2204
        Contact person: Dr. E. G. Avedon, Director
        Founded: 1972

        Purpose: To collect and make available to researchers a machine-
        readable numeric social science data and supplementary documenta-
        tion resulting from studies of leisure behavior conducted by govern-
        ment agencies and individual researchers.   Primarily focuses on
        leisure and outdoor recreation, although also includes fitness and
        sports within the scope of data.

        Services: Reference assistance for in person, mail or telephone
        inquiries; maintain a reading room; provide materials loan ser-
        vices, referral, and consulting services.

        Publications: Bilingual Catalogue of Holdings and Information
        (annually).

607.   Metropolitan Toronto Library, Science and Technology Dept.
        789 Yonge St., Toronto, Ontario
        Canada   M4W 2G8
        (416) 928-5296
        Contact person: Head, Science and Technology Dept.

Purpose: To collect, maintain and make available a collection that
emphasizes sports history and statistics, particularly for Canadian
sports figures. Collection includes an extensive file system of
news clippings, magazine tearsheets, pamphlets, and over 1,200 biographical files on Canadian sports figures.

Services: .Reference assistance provided for in person, telephone
or mail inquiries; allow in-house use of collection; provide copying and limited interlibrary loan.

608. Milwaukee Public Library
      814 W. Wisconsin Ave., Milwaukee, WI 53233
      (414) 278-3000
      Contact person: Henry E. Bates Jr., City Librarian

Purpose: To serve as the major sports resource collection in the
area by collecting, maintaining, and making available newspaper
clippings on local sports and an extensive collection of books;
archival materials and publications from major local sports organizations. Collection also includes material on Olympic Games;
important works on boxing from the turn of the century; all major
sports record books holdings for 20 - 70 years, as well as most
volumes in Spalding's Athletic Library Series and the NCAA.

Services: Reference assistance provided for in person, telephone
or mail inquiries; allow in-house use of the collection; provide
interlibrary loan and copying services.

609. National Athletic Injury/Illness Reporting System (NAIRS)
      The Pennsylvania State University
      131 White Bldg., University Park, PA 16802
      (814) 865-9593
      Contact person: William Buckley, Director
      Founded: 1974

Purpose: To provide a mechanism for the collection and retrieval
of information and statistics on injuries and illnesses incurred
by male and female participants in sports. To maintain a repository of nationally uniform current data for periodic epidemiologi-
cal analysis. To serve as a resource to decision-makers and quali-
fied investigators for research-worthy information.

Services: For those institutions with an organized sports program
or activities who enroll, the services provided are: 1) monthly
reports of statistical tables depicting the enrollee institution's
injury picture to date and 2) ad-hoc reports at the end of a season that re-package the data. The services are also available to
any sports governance agency and, depending on workload and staf-
fing, to other interested individuals.

610. National Federation of State High School Associations
      P. O. Box 20626, 11724 Plaza Circle, Kansas City, MO 64195
      (816) 464-5400
      Contact person: Brice Durbin, Director
      Founded: 1922

Purpose: Collect and make available resources on the subjects of high school sports, sports administration and coaching. The collection consists of about 2,000 books, 500 journals and 350 audiovisual materials.

Services: Reference assistance provided for in person, mail or telephone inquiries; allow in-house use of document collection; and provide material loan, referral, and consulting services.

Publications: Rule books for 16 sports (annually), officials' examinations by sport (annually), Interscholastic Athletic Administration (quarterly).

611.   Nova Scotia Sport Heritage Centre, Olympic Library Hall of Fame and
          Sports Museum
       5516 Spring Garden Road, Halifax, Nova Scotia
       Canada B3J 3G6
       (902) 425-5450
       Contact person: Marlene M. Mullenger, Manager
       Founded: 1977

Purpose: To collect, organize and make available about 1,200 English language documents pertaining primarily to sport coaching and instruction. To maintain a specialized collection of newspaper clippings documenting Nova Scotia sport.

Services: Provide in person, mail or telephone reference assistance; allow in-house use of collection; provide material loan, photocopying, and referral services.

612.   Planning and Technical Services Section, Ministry of Culture and
          Recreation
       77 Bloor St. West, 2nd floor, Toronto, Ontario
       Canada M7A 2R9
       (416) 965-0322
       Contact person: John Shipman, Technical Researcher
       Founded: 1975

Purpose: To collect, organize, and make available research and information support for the construction of physical recreation facilities. The collection includes over 500 books; 15 journals; 1,000 unpublished reports; 2,000 slides; and numerous clippings and pamphlets on the planning, design, construction and operation of arenas, swimming pools, gymnasiums, sports complexes, tracks, playing fields, ski areas, indoor and outdoor courts, etc.

Services: Reference assistance provided for in person, mail or telephone inquiries; allow in-house use of document collection; material loan services, photocopying, and bibliographic searching assistance available; and provide referral and counseling services.

Publications: Newsletter, Facility Fundamentals Recreation Facilities Index (annually).

Access: Ontario residents only.

613. SIR/CAR - University of Windsor Sport Archives of the Sports In-
        stitute for Research/Change Agent Research Sport Archives, Leddy
        Library, University of Windsor
      Windsor, Ontario
      Canada N9B 3P4
      (519) 253-4232, ext. 661
      Contact person: Dr. Dick Moriarty, Director
      Founded: 1971

      Purpose: To house and make accessible to scholars and professional
      practitioners archives, documents, and audio-visual resources for
      about 1,200 items on school sport, amateur athletics, and violence
      in sport. Collection includes unpublished reports, audio-visual
      materials, machine-readable survey data and photographs. Rare
      holdings include minutes of the Canadian Intercollegiate Athletic
      Union from 1906 to present, records of the Central Canada Inter-
      collegiate Football Conference, and comparative Canadian-American
      documents on school sport and amateur athletics.

      Services: Provide reference assistance for in person, mail, or
      telephone inquiries; allow in-house use of the collection.

614. SIRLS - An Information Retrieval System for the Sociology of Lei-
        sure and Sport
      Faculty of Human Kinetics and Leisure Studies, University of
        Waterloo
      Waterloo, Ontario
      Canada N2L 3G1
      (519) 885-1211, ext. 2560
      Contact person: Dr. G. S. Kenyon, Director
      Founded: 1971

      Purpose: Affiliated with the Canadian Working Group in Sport and
      Leisure Documentation, the Centre seeks to identify, collect, in-
      dex, and abstract documentation relating to the social science
      aspects of sport and leisure, and to maintain a computerized bib-
      liographic data base. Collection consists of books, journal arti-
      cles, government reports, unpublished documents, and theses and
      dissertations.

      Services: Reference assistance provided for in person, mail or
      telephone inquiries; allow in-house use of collection; computer-
      ized searches on-demand; referral services; photocopying and docu-
      ment delivery services provided.

      Publications: In conjunction with Elsevier Pub. Co. produces So-
      ciology of Leisure and Sports Abstracts (quarterly) (see #555).

615. Sport and Leisure Resource Centre for Special Populations
      Department of Recreation, University of Waterloo
      415 Phillip St., Waterloo, Ontario
      Canada N2L 3G1
      (519) 885-4721
      Contact person: Dr. Joseph Levy, Director
      Founded: 1976

Purpose: To identify, retrieve, organize and disseminate information relevant to the comprehension, planning, implementation, and
evaluation of sport and leisure services for special populations.
To compile, edit, and publish materials relevant to the delivery
of sport and leisure services for special populations. To provide
consultation and research assistance to practitioners.

Services: Allow in-house access to a collection of documents composed of about 16,000 publications; reference assistance for in
person, mail, or telephone inquiries; provide material loan services and referral services; and provide computerized literature
searching.

Publications: Resource Centre Library Catalogue (bienially),
Resource Centre Audio-Visual (annually), Content Pages of Journals
(monthly)

Access: Restricted to Ontario residents.

616.   Sport Information Resource Centre
        333 River Rd., Ottawa, Ontario
        Canada   K1L 8B9
        (613) 746-5357
        Contact person: Gilles Chiasson, Director
        Founded: 1973

Purpose: To identify, collect, and make available a comprehensive
collection of scientific and practical sport-specific periodical
literature and a representative collection of monographic literature for the fields of sport, physical education and recreation.
Collection consists of over 13,000 books; 1,000 journals; and
50,000 journal articles, of which 84% of the material is in English,
5% in French, and 11% in other languages.

Services: Reference assistance provided for in person, mail, or
telephone inquiries; in-house use of collection allowed; material
loan and photocopying services provided; document delivery service
for some materials; computerized bibliographic literature searching
on-demand; referral and consulting services provided.

Publications: Sport and Recreation Index (monthly), Sport Bibliography. 8 vol. 1981.

617.   Sports Research Institute, Sports Research Building
        Pennsylvania State University, University Park, PA   16802
        (814) 865-9543
        Contact person: C. A. Morehouse, Director

Purpose: To carry out research and disseminate findings on prob-
lems related to competitive sport, with an emphasis on sport safety. As an integral unit of the College of Health, Physical Education and Recreation, this institute cooperates with Penn State's
Biomechanics Laboratory and other related research operations on
campus.

Services: Allows access for professionals and serious researchers to a reading room of about 250 volumes of research reports, reprints, and other materials on all phases of sports performance, including interdisciplinary evaluation and testing of athletes, apparatus, and sports equipment.

Access: By request only.

618. University of Illinois, Urbana-Champaign, Applied Life Studies
         Library
      146 Main Library, Urbana, IL   61801
      (217) 333-3615
      Contact person: M. Jean Armstrong, Librarian

Purpose: To collect, maintain, and make available a fairly comprehensive collection of books and periodicals on all aspects of physical education, as well as good coverage of general books on sports. (Other fields in applied life sciences also included in this departmental library.)

Services: Reference assistance provided for in person, telephone or mail inquiries; provide copying and interlibrary loan services; and allow in-house use of the collection. A separate book catalog of the collection is available (see #373).

619. University of Montreal, Physical Education Library
      C. P. 6128, Succursale "A," Montreal, Quebec
      Canada   H3C 3J7
      (514) 343-6765
      Contact person: Mrs. Lise Mayrand, Librarian
      Founded: 1966

Purpose: To collect, organize and make available material pertinent to undergraduate and graduate studies in the fields of physical education, sport, recreation, leisure, physiology of exercise, biomechanics, and social science aspects of sport. Collection consists of over 28,000 items -- 60% in English, 35% in French, with the remainder in other languages. Books, periodicals and microform materials are included in the collection.

Services: Reference assistance provided for in person, mail or telephone inquiries; allow in-house use of the collection; bibliographic searching available on-demand; and material loan services and photocopying provided.

Publications: Liste des acquisitions (monthly).

620. University of Oregon, College of Health, Physical Education and
         Recreation
      Microform Publications
      Eugene, OR   97403
      (503) 686-4117
      Contact person: Dr. Jan Broekhoff, Director
      Founded: 1949

Purpose: To collect and make available in microfiche unpublished research materials of national significance, particularly doctoral dissertations and masters theses, as well as scholarly books and journals which are out of print.

Services: Reference assistance for in person, mail or telephone inquiries; in-house use of collection; and microfilm/microfiche copies provided for a charge.

Publications: Health, Physical Education and Recreation Microform Publications Bulletin (irregular) plus Supplement (see #371).

621. University of North Carolina, Greensboro, Walter Clinton Jackson
         Library
      1000 Spring Garden St., Greensboro, NC 27412
      (919) 379-5880
      Contact person: Emilie W. Mills, Librarian

Purpose: To maintain and made available a collection of historical materials acquired from Wellesley College, dating from the 16th century to the early 1900's. The collection includes about 1,000 pamphlets, early dance books, gymnastics books from as early as the 16th century, and landmark works on all types of physical activity, training, and theory. Emphasis is on the history of physical education for women.

Services: Reference assistance provided for in person and telephone inquiries; in-house use of the collection allowed; and interlibrary loan and copying services provided.

622. University of Notre Dame Libraries
      International Sports and Games Research Collection
      Notre Dame, IN 46556
      (219) 283-6506
      Contact person: Herbert T. Juliano, Curator
      Founded: 1966

Purpose: To collect, organize and make accessible a variety of types of materials and memorabilia relating to the history and development of sport and physical education. Collection consists of over 20,000 books; 1,000 journals; 3,000 audio-visual materials; and 250,000 programs, rule books, guides, schedules, photographs, brochures, newspapers, etc. Rare holdings include 19th century books and periodicals, the Avery Brundage Olympic Archives, and unpublished photographs.

Services: Reference assistance provided for in person, mail or telephone inquiries; allow in-house use of collection; material loan, photocopying, and microfilm/microfiche services provided; bibliographic searching on-demand; and referral, consulting, and research services provided.

Publications: INSPORT Newsletter (semi-annually).

623.   West Chester State College, Francis H. Green Library
       The Allen-Ehinger Collection
       West Chester, PA   19380
       (215) 436-2643
       Contact person: R. Gerald Schoelkopf, Librarian

       Purpose: To collect, maintain, and make available a comprehensive
       collection of over 600 works which are indicative of the develop-
       ment of physical education from 1890-1947.

       Services: Reference assistance provided for in person, mail, or
       telephone inquiries; provide copying and some interlibrary loan
       services; allow in-house use of the collection.

624.   Women's Sports Foundation
       195 Moulton St., San Francisco, CA   94123
       (415) 563-6266
       Contact person: Eva S. Auchincloss, Executive Director
       Founded: 1974

       Purpose: Provides opportunities, facilities, training, and support
       for women in sports and educates the public on women's athletic
       capabilities.

       Services: Sponsors an information and resource center on women's
       sports; maintains a small library; conducts clinics and workshops
       to improve sport skill, technique, and knowledge; provides sport
       camp, scholarships; and maintains International Women's Sports
       Hall of Fame.

       Publications: Women's Sports (monthly), College Scholarship Guide
       (annual).

PERSONAL AUTHOR INDEX

Thomas, Carolyn E., 540
Thompson, Sherley C., 30, 31
Treat, Roger L., 162
Trekell, M., 462
Turkin, Hy, 31
Turner, Mary Ann, 401 (v.3)
Turner, Pearl, 380
Tyler, Martin, 275
Tymeson, G., 502

Van Daalen, Nicholas, 191
  304
Van Tuyl, Barbara, 123
Visek, Vladimir, 340

Wall, Bob, 238
Ward-Thomas, Pat, 190
Washington, Helen, 426
Watman, Melvyn Francis, 323
Watt, Tom, 207
Wells, Ellen B., 118
Weston, Stanley, 88
Williams, J.G.P., 533
Willoughby, David P., 391
Wilson, Heather, 355
Wilt, Fred, 324
Winderbaum, Larry, 241
Wise, Sydney F., 392
Wright, Graeme, 410
Wright, Hal, 3

Zeigler, Earle F., 462
Zeldin, Dick, 305

CORPORATE AUTHOR INDEX

(See also pages 109-112 for
those associations which publish rules.)

TITLE INDEX

SUBJECT INDEX

About the Compilers

BONNIE GRATCH, BETTY CHAN, and JUDY LINGENFELTER are Reference Librarians at the Drake Library of the State University of New York College at Brockport. They also have collaborated on "A Comparison of Five Physical Education Indexes/Abstracts" for *Reference Quarterly* 21 (Fall 1981) 1: 53-60.